4/2000

THE EXOTIC GARDEN

THE EXOTIC GARDEN

Designing with
tropical plants
in almost any climate

RICHARD R. IVERSEN

The Taunton Press

Cover photo: Dency Kane

for fellow enthusiasts

Printed in the United States of America

10 9 8 7 6 5 4 3 2 1

The Taunton Press, Inc., 63 South Main Street, PO Box 5506, Newtown, CT 06470-5506
e-mail: tp@taunton.com

Distributed by Publishers Group West

Library of Congress Cataloging-in-Publication Data

Iversen, Richard R.
     The exotic garden: designing with tropical plants in almost
any climate / Richard R. Iversen.
          p. cm.
     Includes bibliographical references and index.
     ISBN 1-56158-232-8
     1. Landscape gardening.   2. Tropical plants.   I. Title.
SB473.I94   1999
635.9'523—dc21   98—41862
                                                           CIP

ACKNOWLEDGMENTS

First and foremost, I would like to thank Sean Carrington, Jeff Chandler, and John Leach, who fueled my passion for tropical plants when I lived and worked on the Caribbean island of Barbados.

The Tropical Garden at the Department of Ornamental Horticulture's Teaching Garden, The State University of New York at Farmingdale, provided the inspiration for this book. The garden would never have occurred without the efforts of the department's technical staff—Debbie Cassidy, Gary Fischer, and Fred Lingner. Danielle D'Amore joined the staff in 1998 and has been especially dedicated to the garden. As part of their training, many ornamental horticulture students have worked in the garden preparing its soil, planting, and removing plants for winter. Of special note, Georgia Waltzer helped design the 1996 garden, George Prellwitz contributed to the design of the 1997 and 1998 gardens, and Nicholas Fuschino was instrumental in the success of the 1998 garden.

The success of the Tropical Garden at SUNY Farmingdale has been due to the efforts of the Department of Ornamental Horticulture's summer garden interns: Dawn Bartels, James Holtgreven, and Jennifer Joyner-Lebling in 1996; Rosemary DeFilippo, Darren Lee-Pack, and Stephen Noone in 1997; and Patrick Haugen, Nancy Mathisen, and Florence Riccio in 1998.

Friends, colleagues, and students have read parts of the manuscript at various stages of its development and offered their critique: Robert Bartolomei, Paul Fogelberg, James Holtgreven, Alexandra Randall, Rosalie Schindel, and Steve Whitesell. Dean Nichols requires special thanks for his support of, and contributions to, *The Exotic Garden*, as do my mother Ann and sister Bonnie, who have read the manuscript more times than they may have liked!

Much gratitude goes to Peter Eckert for translating my scratchy sketches into artful illustrations and to Dency Kane for her creative camera work. At The Taunton Press, Helen Albert, Cherilyn De Vries, and Peter Chapman accepted my ideas and shaped them into a complete book.

CONTENTS

INTRODUCTION

If your garden is without luster, sometimes disappointing, or even boring, it's time to replace the roses. Turn it into an exotic paradise with plants like banana or bougainvillea, castor bean or canna—in other words, with tropical plants. There's an intoxicating array of tropical plants available, which you can use to create an environment that will dazzle your senses whether you live in New York or New Orleans. Then, a summer garden will start to emerge that evokes images of a holiday to some Caribbean island, and a holiday that doesn't end after a single week.

Gardeners often assume that tropicals can only be grown as houseplants and often have fussy cultural requirements. This simply isn't true. Tropical plants may be novelties in temperate gardens, but they're as easy to grow outdoors in the open air as marigolds and zinnias. You're not moving into the tropics, where you would have to relearn how to garden, you're just bringing the tropics north! You won't require a battalion of new tools or gadgets to begin this exciting and sophisticated gardening venture. All you need is the spade and trowel from your garage. The care and culture of many tropicals, like bananas, is much simpler than that of a hybrid tea rose.

You'll soon discover that tropical plants reward your gardening efforts *fast*, just as annuals do. In a single season your garden will look like an island paradise. A garden of tropical plants peaks in mid to late summer and is still strong in early autumn when other gardens slump. While the effort involved isn't too different from the effort to create any good garden, the end result is unparalleled; it's a walk through the looking glass into a tropical wonderland.

The exotic garden style tames the jungle without sacrificing its magic or mystery. Luxuriant leaves and bold blossoms come together like the lion and the lamb. Vines creep, crawl, and trail with direction, not aimlessly, as they seem to grow in a jungle. Like the complex strata of the tropical rain forest, the exotic garden has layer upon layer of pattern provided by the color, texture, and form of the foliage and flowers. When properly orchestrated, they all harmonize, yet scintillate; colors are brilliant and hot, textures are large and coarse, forms are statuesque.

My fondness for tropical plants blossomed into an obsession when I lived and worked on the Caribbean island of Barbados. As director of Andromeda Botanic Gardens and senior lecturer in tropical horticulture at The University of the West Indies, I grew what northern gardeners consider houseplants outdoors in steamy, sweltering heat and became forever enchanted by their beauty.

The first houseplant I grew as a child, the shrimp plant (named for its crustacean-like flower stem), was a common garden plant in

Barbados. If it grew so easily in the soil of Barbados, why couldn't it grow in the soil of Long Island? I've discovered that it does. When I returned to the State University of New York at Farmingdale, where I am a professor of ornamental horticulture, it soon became obvious to me that I wouldn't be satisfied without a tropical garden. So, turf was lifted, soil prepared, and an array of tropicals was planted outdoors for the summer months. Now students can see "traditional" interior plants grown outside, and once again I can grow tropical plants in the open air, albeit for only half the year.

The Exotic Garden teaches you how to design, install, and maintain summer gardens rich with tropical plants. You'll learn where to position the exotic garden on your homesite, what size and shape the garden should be, and how to prepare its soil. From the glossary of 100 entries you can choose the candidates to create your tropical paradise. I've suggested which plants are best planted together and complemented summertime maintenance procedures with methods to overwinter the plants for next year's garden.

The Exotic Garden is written for gardeners who crave something new and different and, paradoxically, for gardeners who focus on times past, the way gardens used to be. I am both. As you read these pages, the classic design rules will come into sharp focus, and you'll be inspired to garden anew. And not timidly. I want to teach you how to create your own piece of paradise, a complete garden entity unlike your neighbors', no matter how far from the equator it may be.

1 Tropical Plants

*M*ost people know and grow tropical plants only as houseplants, like viny philodendrons or wandering jews. Far removed from the tropics, these plants live in indoor environments where they are protected from the winter's cold. Their roots are confined to containers that sit upon windowsills or beneath artificial lights. In the interior environment, tropical plants are restrained and stunted, like tigers caged in a zoo, and they aren't always pretty.

Tropical plants grow fast and at the end of September are still at their peak of perfection. Shown here in the Tropical Garden at the State University of New York at Farmingdale are, from left to right: banana (*Musa acuminata* 'Dwarf Cavendish'), coleus (*Solenostemon scutellarioides*), variegated pineapple (*Ananas comosus* 'Variegatus'), variegated plectranthus (*Plectranthus forsteri* 'Marginatus'), maroon-leaved hibiscus (*Hibiscus acetosella* 'Red Shield'), and majesty palm (*Ravenea rivularis*).

Free tropical plants from the constriction of the indoor environment by planting them outdoors for the summer months and they are transformed, like Cinderella. Common houseplants become avant-garde garden plants, tall, strong, and good-looking. Rains wash away last winter's dust, and light levels closer to those of their native tropic environment stimulate growth. Plants grow fast, and in a single season these exotics are at their peak of perfection, as if they were on some Caribbean island. In late summer and early autumn when most traditional garden plants look worn and tired, blasted by the summer heat, tropical plants in temperate gardens get better and better.

Tropical plants are wild plants from the equatorial environments bordered by the Tropic of Cancer in the north and the Tropic of Capricorn in the south, or they are horticultural hybrids and selections of these plants. Within this belt around the center of the globe, tropical plants can originate in cool upland environments, where the air is crisp and clear, or in hot, steamy lowlands. Like forest and grassland plants throughout the United States, tropical plants can be either woody trees, shrubs, vines, or herbaceous perennial and annual plants, but unlike temperate plants, tropical plants are intolerant of frost and cold. Tropical-like plants

The Chinese fan palm (*Livistona chinensis*) is a large indoor plant but a seedling tropical plant. Scarlet salvia hybrids that are grown as summer annuals are shorter than their shrubby wild parents in Brazil.

that are native to lands on the fringe of the tropics, like New Zealand, and are tolerant of temperatures near freezing are sometimes called "subtropical."

The tropical plants on your windowsill are generally smaller than those that grow in the tropics. Rubber plants are trees in the tropics, 200 ft. tall; windowsill plants are rooted cuttings from them. Indoor palms are seedlings of plants that can grow 40 ft. to 60 ft. tall when they are happily sited near the equator. In northern climes we tame tropical trees in conservatories, greenhouses, or atrium displays. Some, such as the benjamin fig (*Ficus benjamina*) or the areca palm (*Chrysalidocarpus lutescens*), survive in shopping malls and hotel lobbies. Many houseplants, such as the Christmas poinsettia, are shrubs that can grow near 10 ft. tall. A few shrubby tropical plants, such as scarlet salvia, are grown as annuals.

Poinsettias are common garden shrubs in Barbados, where they flower when day lengths shorten in December and January. In temperate gardens, when temperatures favor their growth, day lengths are too long for flowering to occur, and when days shorten, temperatures are too cold for poinsettia survival.

In this garden within the tropics, rain-forest plants—golden pothos (*Epipremnum aureum*), philodendron, and bromeliads—grow naturally.

Tropical Plants in Tropical Environments

When I think of tropical plants my mind conjures images of the rain forest, a lush tropical jungle, so-called because of its abundant rainfall and its constant high humidity. In this wild and luxuriant hothouse, where the air is heavy and difficult to breathe, drought and winter are unknown. Plants are tender and unable to survive dry or cold conditions.

Envision a jungle, a majestic and magical basilica where you are dwarfed by thousands of tree species. Aromas assault and intoxicate; you sense a thick scent of life, and its partner, decay. Tall, straight trunks support branches of large and leathery leaves that allow little light to penetrate down to the forest floor. Few herbaceous plants grow in the darkness; most are found in brighter clearings or along the banks of rivers. In the tops of the trees vigor-

The oyster plant (*Tradescantia spathacea*) grows in savannalike Caribbean environments where the climate changes from warm and wet to hot and dry. If you grow it as a houseplant, give it less water during the winter months.

ous vines and climbing shrubs, called lianas, tangle and hang like cables, from which monkeys swing. Aerial plants, known as epiphytes and including bromeliads, cacti such as the night-blooming cereus, and orchids, attach themselves to branches far above the soil.

Rain forests like these are found in South America's Amazon basin, throughout the East Indies, and in central Africa. In these habitats plant growth isn't limited by lack of water or unfavorable temperatures. Rain falls throughout most of the year, and temperatures hover around 80°F. The perpetual midsummer conditions of the jungle enable plant growth to continue uninterrupted. Luxurious specimens of large-leaved species, like the Swiss cheese plant (*Monstera deliciosa*) or the rubber plant (*Ficus elastica*), develop quickly.

Other kinds of tropical plants come from the grassy savannas that exist north and south of the equatorial rain forest in Africa, where giraffes and elephants roam, and in South America and India. Tropical savanna is grassland, often dotted with flat-topped thorny trees of the pea family, called legumes, and patches of open forest. Some savannas are arid. Savanna environments have three seasons, as the climate changes from warm and wet through cool and dry when the sun is at its lowest to hot and dry. Parched grasses often burn before the rains return. Barbados and other Caribbean islands, where the indigenous forest has been cut, experience this weather pattern.

Plants native to savanna environments, like the Barbados lily (*Hippeastrum puniceum*) or the African gloriosa lily (*Gloriosa superba*), enter a dormancy phase when growth stops during the dry season. In cultivation these plants cannot be kept growing continually like rain-forest plants but must have a dormant period imposed upon them, when water and temperature are reduced, during our winter season.

Tropical Plants in Temperate Gardens

Temperate environments combine seasons of arctic cold with tropic heat. Gardens planted within these environments can roast in summertime yet freeze during the winter months, so tropical plants rarely survive outdoors all year long. To create a tropical garden in a temperate environment you need to live where the night temperature will climb above 55°F during some part of the year. When it does, you can bring tropical plants outdoors and fashion them into an exotic garden.

The former botanical name for the banana, *Musa paradisiaca*, alludes to its Edenic qualities: large leaves, bizarre blossom, and sweet fruit.

fruits. And it is possible to create an exotic garden even where ice and snow cover the ground six months of the year!

Many gardeners toil over gardens all year long, only to enjoy brief bursts of color. Enter an exotic garden, where tropical flowers and foliage provide exotic arrangements for the senses all season long. Hibiscus unfold, palm trees sway, and banana plants grow tall. It's a garden where foliage is king and on the throne until the first frost.

Colors, textures, habits, and fragrances of tropical plants seem endless. Foliage and form are as flamboyant as flowers. Some leaves are larger than umbrellas, while others are as stiff as a spear. The best arrangement of tropical foliage plants is one that contains the most variety of color, texture, and form, as in any garden where massive rugged leaves and slender wandlike plants are grown together. The impressions of rugged beauty and slender gracefulness are then intensified by their contrast.

For me, one of the great joys in growing tropical plants is witnessing their absurd scale. Giant plants with gigantic leaves, like Jack's beanstalk, are fun and defy our prim garden conventions. But they don't need large spaces to look good. One of the best and most popular uses of tropical plants is in summertime patio containers. Within their confines you can grow a single specimen of a tropical tree, shrub, or vine, as well as an entire garden in miniature.

An exotic garden is a celebration of the diversity of the tropics. It's a spicy style that calls to mind faraway havens where balmy breezes blow and temperatures are kind. Paradise found. It's my vision of Eden, luxuriant with different kinds of large and lush leaves, bizarre and brilliant blossoms, and, of course, sweet

For greatest impact, I like to grow tropical plants in a special garden by themselves. Then a totally tropic environment emerges. Tropical foliage plants form a good team with tropical bedding plants, such as coleus, wax begonias, and impatiens. They've been planted together in lawn beds since the middle of the

Tropical plants don't need large spaces to look good. Houseplants vacationing outdoors as patio plants can make an intimate exotic arrangement. From left to right: croton (*Codiaeum variegatum pictum*), bromeliad, pygmy date palm (*Phoenix roebelinii*), and myers asparagus fern (*Asparagus densiflorus* 'Myersii').

19th century. And some tropical plants can be combined successfully with nontropical, winter-hardy plants in a mixed perennial border where you may mistake them for hardy plants.

Unique needs of tropical plants in temperate gardens

Not all tropical plants are as easy to grow as bananas or castor beans, nor do they all grow so quickly. For example, orchids reward fastidious care slowly wherever they are grown. Plants like poinsettia flower only after the day length naturally shortens in the autumn, when it is time to put the exotic garden to bed. They need the continuous protection provided by a glasshouse or warm windowsill.

Since tropical plants originate in various kinds of tropic environments, they have varying temperature and water requirements for their optimal growth, which will dictate your planting and overwintering strategy. There isn't one general rule for the successful culture of all tropical plants since there isn't one general tropical plant. Some like their surrounding atmosphere to be hot and humid, others prefer it cool and dry.

It's not necessary, nor is it possible, for your temperate garden to mimic all tropic environments. Just because a plant may be native to the rain forest doesn't mean it requires rain-forest conditions in order to grow; you don't need a jungle to grow plants from the jungle. The Swiss cheese plant hails from the banks of jungle rivers yet grows successfully in the lobbies of banks. It continually astounds me how tropical plants can adapt to various environmental conditions. The plants I'm suggesting you cultivate are as easy to plant and grow outdoors as a tomato or a zucchini.

The ornamental sweet potato, *Ipomoea batatus* 'Margarita', (lower right) becomes a robust groundcover when supplemented with liquid fertilizer. Cuttings from it can be easily rooted and overwintered on a sunny windowsill.

While many tropical plants are rare and endangered species, those that I list in this book can all be found in the American nursery trade. A few you'll have to search for; others stare at you along the grocery-store checkouts. In late May or early June you'll plant them in a richly prepared, fertile, and loamy garden soil. It should be loose and friable, not rough and rocky, just like the soil for your vegetables. Dark, deep, and drained organic soils that absorb solar heat in the spring will warm up fast and foster good root growth.

Once the tropicals are planted, you need to water and feed them during the summer months. Many kinds grown for foliage alone are heavy feeders and respond dramatically to liquid fertilizers applied every week or two during June and July. Then marvel at the fruits of your labor! In October, when the gardening season starts to draw to a close, prepare to overwinter your tropical plants in a frost-free environment. Some species can be dug and potted, and spend the winter in a cold garage (at about 40°F). Others might return to the comfort of your windowsill (either the entire parent plant or just a cutting from it). Still others may be left in the ground to succumb to winter and be repurchased from garden centers the following spring. The exotic-plant glossary at the end of this book expounds on the essentials of 100 tropical plants, telling you how to grow and use each of them successfully.

Exotic gardens are more than just tropical plants. To use them to their best advantage, plants need to be arranged within a designed space and on a carefully considered site. To make the best garden you must first find the best site on your property for that garden. Cultural requirements of tropical plants are only one factor to consider; the garden site is also determined by the topography and ecology of the property, as well as by the architecture of the residence.

Tropical plants will benefit from a protected site that buffers strong and dry wind. Some leaves tear or desiccate in exposed conditions. Your house or an enclosed garden (see chapter 3) can act as a perfect windbreak. Like most flowering plants, tropicals require sunshine for at least half a day, so gardens on the south, west, or east side of your house are best. However, some species are content with or require dappled shade. If your property is shady, you'll need to learn which tropicals will grow there to achieve an exotic effect.

After the best site is chosen, you can formulate planting spaces, such as borders or beds, using the classic rules of proportion and balance, either symmetric or asymmetric. This crucial stage sets the garden's foundation.

Historic uses of tropical plants in temperate gardens

Taming jungles for nontropical climates isn't an entirely new concept. Beautiful-leaved tropical plants were the stylish embellishment to colorful lawn beds in the last quarter of the 19th century in Europe and America.

In his 1870 book *New and Rare Beautiful-leaved Plants*, Shirley Hibberd, the eminent English gardener, espoused the use of tropical foliage plants either indoors, under glass, or outside in gardens. He wrote the book in response to Edward Lowe's 1861 work, *Beautiful Leaved*

Plants, which also praised the beauty of foliage. Hibberd convinced his readers that the passion for collecting and cultivating fine-foliage plants was unlikely to be transient because sumptuous leaves are permanent, whereas flowers are temporary.

The fashion for tropical foliage began in mid-19th-century European gardens, most notably in public parks in and around Paris, before succeeding in England's Battersea Park

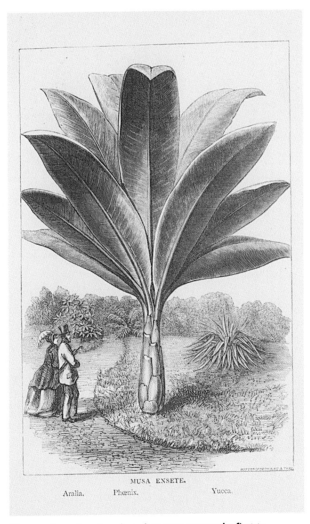

MUSA ENSETE.

Aralia.   Phœnix.   Yucca.

Nineteenth-century French gardens were among the first to incorporate tropical foliage plants. (From *Gleanings From French Gardens*, by William Robinson, London, 1868.)

The Abyssinian banana (*Ensete ventricosum* 'Maurelii') is the noblest of all tropical plants to be used in an exotic garden.

around 1870. Tender tropical plants with large foliage or stately habit were introduced into open-air formal flower gardens during the summer months. This "subtropical garden" provided a glimpse of luxuriant tropical vegetation, otherwise unobtainable in northern climates. Subtropical gardening came to mean the culture of plants with large or remarkable foliage in association with short, colorful bedding plants; and most gardeners at that time agreed that the best arrangements of tropical plants were those that contained the most variety of color, texture, and form.

William Robinson, the notoriously outspoken English journalist best known for the wild garden, altered the subtropical garden in an informal, picturesque way. He planted beautiful large-leaved forms naturally, believing that gardens, without becoming a wilderness, should have all the grace, beauty, shade, relief, and irregularity of nature. In the 1870s Robinson became an advocate for plants with large and handsome leaves, noble habit, or graceful port to alleviate the monotony of single-color gardens.

According to Robinson, the greatest and noblest of all plants to be used in the flower garden is the Abyssinian banana (*Ensete ventricosum*). The magnificent leaves of this plant withstand rain and storms without laceration, and it is easy to overwinter in the drought and heat of a living room. America's premier horticulturist, Liberty Hyde Bailey, noted in 1900 that "its immense leaves arching out from the top of the stalk give an effect of tropical luxuriance. As decorative plants in landscape gardening few subjects equal the banana, and as they are of easy growth, their cultivation in temperate climates is on the increase." In the last decades of the 19th and the first decades of the 20th centuries, America's garden decoration was to include bananas growing within subtropical beds.

The Victorian subtropical bedding style in America remained popular in part due to the influential writings of Peter Henderson, a tireless florist and seedsman who located his market-garden business in Jersey City, New Jersey. *Practical Floriculture,* first published for professional florists in 1869, was revised in 1887 and again in 1903. Similarly, three editions of *Gardening for Pleasure* (1875, 1887, and 1906) guided amateurs in making their flower gardens. In all publications Henderson contrasted planting borders with beds. Old-fashioned long borders, 4 ft. to 6 ft. wide, were promiscuously interspersed with hardy herbaceous plants, tall at the back graduating to lower-growing sorts in front, although mixed borders could also contain a heterogeneous grouping of all kinds of tropical plants arranged similarly.

But it was the "modern" style bed, viewed from all sides, that Peter Henderson most admired (see chapter 4). These beds were planted with rings of tropical plants that sloped downward from the highest in the middle to shorter kinds at the front edge or lowest point to create a three-dimensional pyramid. Henderson first saw such massed plantings in England on visits in 1872 and 1885. Filled with tropical castor beans that grow 10 ft. to 12 ft. tall in one season, large-leaved tropical "tanyah" or elephant's ears, and tropical annual amaranths, tropical beds were more interesting to Henderson than a promiscuous perennial border could ever be.

At Andromeda Botanic Gardens, Barbados, sago palms (*Cycas revoluta*) and yuccas (*Yucca elephantipes*) are arranged in an informal, picturesque way that would have pleased William Robinson.

2

Designing with Tropical Plants

*P*lopping a banana plant into the soil next to an azalea may look exotic, but it doesn't make an exotic garden. To design an exotic garden you need to arrange tropical plants artistically within a border or bed, not just group them randomly. Throughout this design process, you must keep in mind three elements: color, texture, and form. They are the tools you'll use to select and combine plants that harmonize and enhance each other, to create a tropical paradise rather than a chaotic jungle.

The hot, calypso colors in Audrey Thomas's Barbados garden do not weaken in the intense tropic sunlight but are strong and stimulating.

Color

Color is the main attraction in any garden. The first, and sometimes the only, impression people have of a garden comes from their reaction to the color scheme. Since color conveys the mood of a garden, which can be anything from peaceful and tranquil to riotous and fun, choosing the color scheme is critical. Do you want to be soothed or swept away, calmed or aroused? Color can make either option possible.

When used properly, color unifies the entire garden composition. If the color of one plant relates to that of its neighbors, the garden starts to emerge as a single idea, creating unity and smoothing disparate edges. One of the easiest ways to unify a garden is to use theme colors, such as a garden devoted to red flowers and foliage or another dominated by yellow, orange, and yellowish-orange blossoms. But sometimes you don't want the entire garden to blend together totally; otherwise, it may become monotonous. In these instances, using primary or complementary colors will spice up the composition and provide accent. When you

Cool-colored tropicals (*Tibouchina urvilleana*, *Tradescantia pallida* 'Purple Heart', and *Heliotropium arborescens*), salvia, and dusty miller fade into the distance at Longwood Gardens, Kennett Square, Pennsylvania.

understand how to blend colors to unify the garden and how to contrast them for accent, you'll understand how to create the best plant combinations and the best exotic garden.

Setting the mood

Light is the source of color. It travels to your eyes in waves of different lengths, each length perceived by your eye as a different color. When light passes through a prism, the waves become sorted into a spectrum, or a rainbow, with the colors arranged in the order of their wavelength from red, the longest, to violet, the shortest. These colors are termed "hues" or the "fundamental colors." They are clear and pure, not faded by the addition of white

or darkened by the addition of black. The spectrum is our basis for understanding color relationships and color harmony.

Colors formed from long wavelengths—reds, oranges, and yellows—are associated with heat and are termed "warm" or "hot" colors. They are the fiery elements in your composition. By contrast, colors of short wavelengths—greens, blues, and violets—are cool in their associations, like water, ice, or shadow. Warm and cool colors possess intrinsic properties important to the garden designer. If the space is too large, hot colors shrink it down, bringing distant scenes closer. Red carries across distances quicker and crisper than blue and excites the eye faster. It advances aggressively, speeds the pulse, and stimulates the senses into action.

Use red for accent—it will jump at you and be seen first.

Warm colors change less than cool colors in waning light and shadows, and they weaken less in bright sunshine. Use them to set the mood: primitive and passionate, lively and noisy. Tropical. The calypso colors of hibiscus and bougainvillea stimulate and arouse emotions. Like a steel drum band, when you play with hot colors, quietness and subtlety are in short supply.

Cool colors are tranquil, reserved, and restrained. They are peaceful and soothing. Icy cold blue retreats into the heavens, like the pale azure skies of Leonardo da Vinci's landscapes that seem to go on forever as they fade into the distance. Because of this property, cool colors are used to make a small space appear larger. In my Barbados garden next to the beach, the sky-blue flowers of plumbago planted in the shadows of coconut palms disappeared into the turquoise sea beyond, as if the sky met the sea at some distant horizon. If I wanted to see them, I had to be near them. Use blue to create the mysterious mood of the sea.

The three primary colors—red, yellow, and blue—cannot be produced by mixing other color pigments. Their strength stimulates your eyes but may also overwhelm. When primary pigments are mixed with each other, the secondary colors—orange, green, and violet—are formed. The more pure primary and secondary hues you use in a composition, the greater the chance that they will react too strongly with each other, so it's best not to use them all together. If you do, dilute them with more neutral colors. The Victorians created huge flower beds where greater quantities of duller and more neutral tertiary colors were combined with fewer pure primary and secondary hues. Artists can produce more neutral tertiary

colors by mixing secondary pigments, but gardeners need to seek plants that nature (or genetic engineers!) imbued with tertiary color.

Strong contrasts

A tool to determine color harmony is the color wheel, an arrangement of the spectral colors into a circle. Pairs of colors directly opposite each other on the wheel are termed complementary. They represent the greatest possible contrast of color, one that is balanced and harmonious. Nature often combines opposite colors in a single flower, as in the orange and blue bird-of-paradise blossom. You can use complementary colors as the Victorians did to create a flower bed with the greatest color contrast and visual impact.

The extreme contrast of complementary colors increases the brilliance of each of the two colors

The Color Wheel

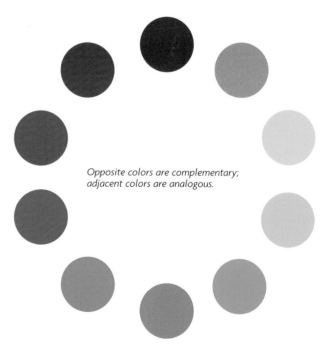

Opposite colors are complementary; adjacent colors are analogous.

Complementary colors can be found in a single flower, like the orange and blue bird-of-paradise blossom (*Strelitzia reginae*).

A complementary effect occurs when yellowish and purplish foliages (*Sanchezia speciosa*, *Alpinia zerumbet* 'Variegata', *Helichrysum petiolare* 'Limelight', and *Tradescantia pallida* 'Purple Heart') come together.

when they are placed side by side. For instance, yellow seems more intense when placed beside its complement violet than when seen against green. Gardeners in northern climes can most likely visualize the intensity of yellow forsythia when it's in combination with the violet 'PJM' rhododendron in the spring landscape. Or basket-of-gold seems brighter in the rockery when purple rock cress is nearby. Witness a similar effect in a tropical garden when yellow flowers of the viny allamanda mingle through

the purple leaves of *Pseuderanthemum atropurpureum*, or when *Tradescantia pallida* 'Purple Heart' trails into yellow lantana, or simply when yellow and purplish foliages come together. If you crave loud colors, using equal quantities of complementary colors will satisfy your craving.

If you prefer something slightly quieter, choose one color of a complementary pair to dominate a planting scheme. Then introduce the second color more sparingly for accent; for example, plant one specimen of purple *Tibouchina* as an accent in a bed of yellow lantana. If this is still too intense for your taste, decrease the accent quality by contrasting flowers with paler color values, like a pastel yellow lantana cultivar with the lavender trailing lantana.

At Montrose Gardens, analogous hot-color flowers (*Tithonia rotundifolia, Gomphrena* 'Strawberry Fields', and *Zinnia angustifolia*) blend into each other and are intensified by burgundy foliage.

Subtle contrasts

Neighboring hues on the color wheel are called adjacent or analogous. Progressions, or gradations, from one hue into the next will form a quiet and restful color harmony, one that is simple, yet successful. A garden planted with warm yellow colors that blend through yellow-orange into orange is cheerful and pleasing because these colors are closely positioned on the color wheel (see the photo at left). Observe the colors of a single flower and notice how they move from one hue into the next. In nature, colors come alive because of the infinite amount of color gradation within them. Your tropical garden will also come alive if you choose a color scheme with the greatest amount of color gradation possible.

Monochromatic, or single-color, gardens occur when one dominant hue is accompanied by only the very closest hues next to it on the color wheel (and tints and shades of them). Monochromatics are among the safest color schemes; there are no contrasts. All colors grade naturally from one into the next, so a successful monochromatic garden is easy to create. In this composition, your eyes become saturated by only one hue and its tints and shades. Since there are no contrasting colors, it is necessary to contrast textures and forms. Some of the most effective plant combinations occur when plants of similar flower and leaf colors but of opposing sizes and shapes are planted together.

Tints are dilutions of a spectral hue with white. Most flower colors are a tint of something. Color harmonies occur when single hues are combined with their tints, like violet and lavender or orange and apricot. In the tropical garden, try placing the purplish-foliage plants *Strobilanthes dyerianus* or *Tradescantia pallida*

Right: The purplish foliage of Persian shield (*Strobilanthes dyerianus*) and wandering jew (*Tradescantia zebrina*) blends together the pink flowers of Brazilian plume (*Justicia carnea*), *Fuchsia* 'Mrs J. D. Fredericks', and New Guinea impatiens.

Below: The lavender flowers of *Lantana montevidensis* are a tint of the purplish foliage of *Tradescantia pallida* 'Purple Heart'.

Below right: Matching colors and contrasting textures of *Justicia carnea*'s flowers and caladium's foliage create an interesting monochromatic plant combination.

It is not unusual to find tropical plants with yellowish or burgundy-colored leaves. They are as important as flower colors to the design of tropical gardens.

The burgundy foliage color of *Dahlia* 'Ellen Houston' is a shade of its red-hued flowers.

'Purple Heart' next to the lavender flowers of *Lantana montevidensis*.

Shades of a spectral hue form when the hue is darkened. In nature, shades are often found in foliage. Burgundy and bronze leaves are shades of red and are different from purplish foliage, which is a shade of purple. Dark gold vegetation is a shade of yellow. Occasionally, plants present an artful package of both a shade and its appropriate hue, like the bronze-leaved and red-flowered *Canna* 'Ambassador' and *Dahlia* 'Ellen Houston'. Shades also form in the garden when shadows fall upon bright colors.

Color in foliage

In the tropical garden, foliage colored other than green—burgundy, bronze, purplish, gold, or gray—is as important as colored flowers. Leaves remain colorful when flowers fail. Temperate gardeners frequently ignore foliage colors when they design gardens, but when they use tropical plants, they can't. Fabulous foliage, often as gold as a daffodil or as red as a rose, is one of the great assets of tropicals; and some plants, like croton, have leaves that are both gold and red!

Purplish- or burgundy-foliage plants can unify a color palette. Plants with leaves that are a shade of purple, like many species of *Tradescantia,* the purple waffle, or the Persian shield, blend together analogous cool-color flowers—sky blue, lavender, rose, pink, or purple. Try a combination of these plants with *Plumbago auriculata, Lantana montevidensis,* the elfin plant (*Cuphea hyssopifolia*), pink *Pentas lanceolata,* the Brazilian glory bush (*Tibouchina urvilleana*), or heliotrope to see it happen.

Impressionistic effects of light and shadow occur when you use plants with deep-shaded foliage, like *Hibiscus acetosella* 'Red Shield' or *Alternanthera dentata* 'Rubiginosa'. They recede into the background to create a sense of depth. Use them to make the space seem larger than it is. By surprise, when burgundy or bronze foliage contrasts with hot colors—yellow, gold, orange, or red—the colors are intensified and made even hotter (as shown in the photo at right). As the burgundy or bronze foliage inches backward, the hot colors elevate forward until you can feel the heat radiate, as when *Hibiscus acetosella* 'Red Shield' is grown near the annual *Cosmos sulphureus* or red and orange canna cultivars.

To be certain the color effects you envision will actually materialize in your garden, snip leaf and flower samples and place them next to each other, as if in a floral arrangement. To confirm that the proposed palette follows color theory correctly, match your collage of cut plant parts to the color wheel. If the effects are truly harmonious and what you are looking for, you are ready to arrange them into a garden plan.

Burgundy or bronze foliage intensifies hot colors (*Canna* 'Red King Humbert', *Hibiscus acetosella* 'Red Shield').

Texture

Tropical plants display an amazing variety of texture, which is what I react to most in the tropical garden. I use texture extensively, and not timidly, to create sensational plant arrangements that look as tropical as those along the Amazon River. Texture is as important in the garden as color, yet I suspect most people don't fully understand what it is all about.

Texture is most often associated with the weave of fabric, where it is determined by the size and spacing of the threads. Thin and tightly arranged threads produce a fine-textured weave, whereas thick and loosely woven threads are coarse. In the context of plants, texture refers to the size, shape, and surface quality of their parts, like leaves or flowers, and how nature positioned them upon a twig, branch, or stem, not to the size or shape of the entire plant, which is its form (see p. 34).

Henri Rousseau, *Fight between a Tiger and a Buffalo*, 1908, Hermitage Museum, St. Petersburg, Russia. The mystery and secrets that lurk in the depth of Rousseau's naive jungle are attributable to texture: Coarse-textured foliage, like banana and ginger, is in the foreground, layered over finer-textured citrus trees.

Fine textures

Small leaves or leaflets have a fine texture. If the edge of a leaf or leaflet is lobed or dissected—for example, the florist leather fern—the effect is finer. Lobed or dissected leaves or leaflets supported by long and slender stalks, like those of a maidenhair fern, are even airier. They become animated with the will of the wind. The finest texture results when slender-stalked, small, lobed or dissected leaves or leaflets are widely spaced upon the plant. Then, shadows form between the leaves or leaflets to make them appear soft and delicate. Fine textures, like cool colors and burgundy foliage, make small spaces seem larger when they are strategically placed within garden bays and recesses. When used in conjunction with coarse textures, and usually behind them, they extend the sense of depth.

Foliage Texture

Fine

Maidenhair fern (*Adiantum* sp.)

Medium

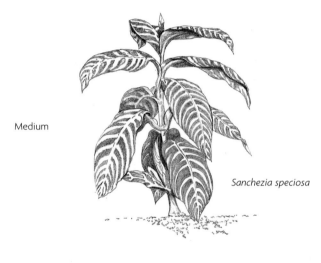

Sanchezia speciosa

The smaller leaves of *Myrtus communis* 'Variegata' (left) have a finer texture than the larger leaves of *Plectranthus forsteri* 'Marginatus' (right).

Coarse

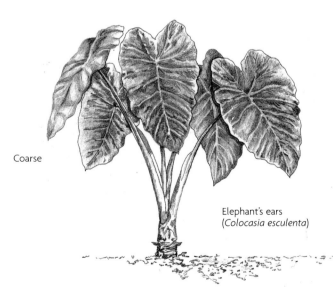

Elephant's ears
(*Colocasia esculenta*)

Plants native to tropical savannas tend to have finer textures than those native to tropical rain forests. The leaves of most grasses are narrow and fine, as are the thorny pea-family trees, the legumes, that grow on the open savanna. Their leaves are frequently dissected and compound, like the common mimosa tree that is planted throughout the American South.

Coarse textures

Large, round, or oval leaves, like those of *Colocasia esculenta,* appear coarse and robust (see the photo at left below). When the leaves are rigid upon a branch and set apart from each other, the coarseness is magnified, as exemplified by the common rubber plant. Appendages to a leaf, such as bristles or hairs, add coarseness, whereas glossy leaves reflect the light, sparkle, and appear smaller. Coarse textures pounce at you. There is nothing dainty or doilylike about them. They create bold moods and effects like those of hot colors and should be used similarly. And when coarse textures are used with hot colors, the garden sizzles—just like the tropics.

In tropical environments where water is always available, large leaves are efficient photosynthetic organs, so plants native to the moist tropics, like *Monstera deliciosa* and other aroids, are often monstrous and grow out of proportion. In a garden that is emulating these tropi-

Heat radiates when large, variegated leaves (*Alpinia zerumbet* 'Variegata') and hot flower colors (*Canna* 'Lucifer') come together.

There's nothing dainty and doilylike about the coarse-textured aroid, elephant's ears. The leaves pounce at you!

cal effects, coarse-textured foliage is essential, and it often takes precedence over flowers. Robust leaves pulsate and are quick to excite and add accent. They exude exoticism!

I'm generous with my use of large-leaved plants like canna, aroids such as elephant's ears, Chinese fan palms, or, my favorite, the banana. They jump at you, but the effect is uniquely tropical. In the tropics coarse textures greet you wherever you turn, making the tropical garden a fun place to be in. It's in defiance of the prim garden convention that uses coarse texture sparingly.

Texture, just like color, can be manipulated within gardens to create harmony or discord.

Using similar textures throughout a garden unifies it into a harmonious composition, but one that is often monotonous. Position plants of dissimilar textures next to each other and startling and spicy contrasts occur and highlight one another. Combine the flat sedge (*Cyperus alternifolius*) with elephant's ears (*Colocasia esculenta* and *Alocasia macrorrhiza*), as shown in the photo at right below. Both plants are the same color and thrive in damp conditions, yet their leaf size and shape, and resultant texture, are in sharp opposition. The sedge is tall and slender, its leaves are narrow and radiate from the top of the triangular stem to resemble the ribs of an umbrella, while those of elephant's ears are wide and round. Together, they look like Laurel and Hardy and form a dramatic duo in the garden.

The coarse canna-like foliage of *Curcuma zedoaria*, decorated with a purplish-red stripe along its midvein, is combined with the large, purplish-red-foliaged coleus 'Solar Sunrise' and the small, red-flowered *Jatropha integerrima*.

The leaves of flat sedge (*Cyperus alternifolius*) and elephant's ears (*Colocasia esculenta*) are both a similar shade of green but their textures contrast.

An Essential Coarse-Textured Pair

Tropical gardens are textural gardens, and the most striking textural effects come from two of the commonest and easiest to grow tropical plants: bananas and palms.

A tropical garden isn't complete without the coarse foliage and floral effects of at least one banana plant. I use several. They are huge herbaceous plants (not trees), that grow from an underground corm, similar to crocus. What appears to be the tree "trunk" are actually the leaf bases, or sheaths, clasped together into a stemlike structure, which quickly becomes thick and stocky. Tightly rolled new leaves push their way upwards through the stem, emerge, and expand into the large and coarse leaf blades. They range in length from 3 ft. to 10 ft., depending on the variety. Like a chorus of Disney hippopotami, these hefty leaves lighten up as they dance delicately with the breeze. Prominent parallel veins extend from the thick midrib to the leaf margin like the steps of a ladder, but strong winds often rip the leaf blades along their length. The ripped leaves are part of the banana appeal and make the texture appear only slightly finer.

To compound the coarseness of leaves and stem, older banana plants produce flowers as bold and grand as the leaves. From the center of the leafy crown a bizarre and heavy flowering structure,

several feet long, emerges and hangs downward. Bunches of bananas ripen yellow along its length.

Palms, the symbol of the tropics, herald the exotic garden with pageantry. In temperate tropical gardens they rarely produce their small, yet significant, flowers but are grown for foliage textures, which are either coarse or fine. Palm leaves, sometimes called fronds, blend effectively with the

other bold-leaved tropical plants, especially bananas.

Leaves come in two general shapes: fan-shaped (palmate) and feather-shaped (pinnate). Pleated fan-shaped leaves look like a Japanese fan, emerging from the center of the crown and opening into a blade that is more or less circular in outline. Its edge is dissected into segments, the depth of dissection influencing the texture. For example, the leaf

Bananas (*Musa acuminata* 'Dwarf Cavendish') are essential exotics for the tropical garden. They grow fast and without much bother.

margin of the Mediterranean fan palm (*Chamaerops humilis*) is more deeply incised than the Chinese fan palm (*Livistona chinensis*), and therefore its texture is finer. However, the leaf blades of both species are larger than those of most other plants, and they provide the garden with a unique tropical texture. I grow them outdoors in full sun, as they once grew in 19th-century lawn beds (see chapter 4) and still grow in Caribbean gardens.

Mature feather palms have leaf blades 10 ft. to 15 ft. long. Each is cut to the midrib forming leaflets, and leaflet size determines texture. As plants age, the new leaves become larger and the texture becomes coarser, as with the common majesty palm (*Ravenea rivularis*). Young plants produce delicate fronds with narrow leaflets, less than $\frac{1}{2}$ in. wide. Fronds resemble the areca or golden palm (*Chrysalidocarpus lutescens*) but are a richer green. Breezes animate them, sunshine illuminates them, and light is reflected from them, all adding to their delicacy. On mature plants leaflets are wider and fronds appear coarser, reminiscent of the kentia palm (*Howea forsterana*).

Pleated palmate leaves of the Chinese fan palm (*Livistona chinensis*) are roundish and resemble Japanese fans.

Pinnate-leaved palms produce long feather-shaped fronds. Bright red-leaf petioles on the sealing-wax palm (*Cyrtostachys lakka*) make it a choice landscape plant in the tropics.

Form

The shape or outline of a plant is its form or "habit," which is the result of the plant's branching pattern: horizontal, vertical, or bending. It may be distinct and echo geometric forms that are easy to define and name, like rounded spheres, vertical cylinders, or pyramidal cones, or it may be irregular and more difficult to categorize. Some tropical and subtropical plants possess a forceful geometric form; their leaves are as stiff as stems and stand out visually among other plants. When the geometry of branching is sharp and clearly defined, the plant is said to have an "architectural" form.

Architectural forms

Architectural plants may combine several geometric forms, as with *Cordyline indivisa*. Its stiff center stem is upright and vertical, or fastigiate in appearance, but the overall outline formed by the firm, linear leaves that spiral around the stem is strongly spherical (see the drawing at right). Commanding attention, the vertical stem punctuates the garden with exclamation. Upward it travels, connecting the soil with the sky. Stems like this draw attention away from weaker, floppier ones that cannot support themselves and act as ground covers.

Architectural plants are appropriate additions to formal geometric gardens, where they strengthen the architectural design. In these sites, they should be positioned as symmetrically as the borders or beds. Place four specimens at the junction of four corners where pathways intersect to highlight the junction and direct traffic, or use an architectural pair to define the beginning of a path. Architectural specimens emphasize repetition, which is another way to unify the garden composition. When a single strong and tall fastigiate form marches down the length of a border, it establishes a theme and sends a single message.

Tall, spiky plants are also the traditional centerpiece of geometric beds, such as circles cut into the lawn, where they bring height to the

Architectural Form

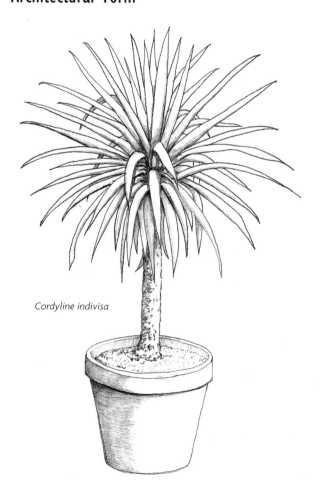

Cordyline indivisa

middle of the bed. If short architectural plants edge a bed, they emphasize its outline and also mask looser forms behind them.

But, most important, architectural plants are accent specimens with strong visual impact. The garden effect they bring about is sculptural. Like crisply carved marble in a museum's courtyard, these indispensable objects energize a tropical border, bed, or container; eyes open and adrenalin begins to flow. The accentuating shape of some tropical species, like *Dracaena marginata* 'Bicolor', is even whimsical (as shown in the photo below). Comical tufts of 12-in.-long linear leaves, often striped white, pink, or red, top leggy stems that twist and turn.

Since architectural plants evoke the strongest reaction, I position them into the design first and then arrange the remaining plants around them. They become the pivots from which all other plants radiate. For the strongest architectural statement, pot these plants into an architectural container instead of planting them directly into the soil. Then site them as architecture within the garden.

The variegated leaf form of the common houseplant *Dracaena marginata* 'Bicolor' is quick to capture attention when planted outdoors. Tufts of stiff linear leaves crown stems that twist and turn as they mature.

Agavaceous Architecture

Plants within the family Agavaceae, like the century plant (*Agave*), *Cordyline*, *Dasylirion*, *Dracaena*, *Furcraea*, New Zealand flax (*Phormium*), the snakeplant (*Sansevieria*), and *Yucca*, are stiff and special, and are among the best architectural plants. *Cordyline indivisa*, one of the commonest (see the drawing on p. 34), is the traditional favorite for sunny lawn beds. As an unbranched spike, 3 ft. to 6 ft. tall, it is the sentinel of the garden. Long lance-shaped leaves spiral around a stiff center stem with complete symmetry and balance. A similar plant, *Cordyline australis* 'Purpurea', combines burgundy foliage with the same dramatic form.

The New Zealand flax (*Phormium*) doesn't produce a central trunk like *Cordyline indivisa,* but its garden effect is similar. Stiff, sword-shaped, linear leaves, 3 ft. to 6 ft. long, are fastigiate and form a vertical accent to punctuate flat plantings. Magnificent bronze, variegated, or glaucousy-green, flat, irislike foliar fans develop from a rhizome beneath the soil.

Furcraea foetida 'Mediopicta' is unique among rigid, upright plants. Luminescent leaves emerge from the heart of the plant in a vertical position. As they mature, the leaves spiral downward until they align themselves horizontally, giving the plant a dramatic hemispherical silhouette. Ice-cream-color stripes, French vanilla and mint-green, alternate on leaves 5 in. wide and

Phormium colensoi 'Maori Sunrise' is used architecturally at Wave Hill, Bronx, New York.

Furcraea foetida 'Mediopicta'.

3 ft. long. The leaf acts as a tub that collects water, where small golden warblers are known to bathe.

Few herbaceous plants are as erect as the species and color-variant cultivars of the common houseplant mother-in-law's tongue or snakeplant (*Sansevieria*). They grow anywhere in anything, in full sun or light shade. Nothing is tougher. Grown outdoors, directly in the soil or as container centerpieces, *Sansevieria* lose their commonness and are among the most vertical of all plants.

Sansevieria trifasciata 'Laurentii'.

It isn't required that architectural plants be members of the family Agavaceae; for example, the stiff and succulent *Aloe vera* in the Liliaceae family is more akin to a lily. But those plants that are related to *Agave* are as strong as steel.

Flexible forms

Plants with an irregular or somewhat ambiguous outline are the architectural plant's antithesis. They are more flexible in the design scheme and become background filler plants or lower ground covers. Since our eyes distinguish one form by its contrast with another, the best way to use a particular form is to highlight it against a different form. The extreme contrast between a rigid architectural outline and the loose and limp flexible forms nearby provides a dramatic climax that stops your eye and drops your jaw. The changing outline of one plant next to its neighbor adds visual interest to the garden composition.

Plant forms change over time

The form of a plant can change as the plant matures, depending on how we use it in the garden or landscape or how we prune it. If we do not contrast one plant form with another, the individual plants blend together and may take a different group form. For example, a single specimen of canna has a tall, vertical, fastigiate stem and its form is cylindrical, but plant a mass of a single variety tight in a bed and the line of the composition changes from vertical to horizontal, since the bed the plants occupy is a horizontal statement upon the landscape. The forms of the individual plants

connect together and change when the plants are viewed as a group.

Pruning, as with topiary, creates new forms or strengthens existing ones. Some flexible forms can be sheared into a rounded sphere or a pyramidal cone, as can happen when you prune *Abutilon pictum* 'Thompsonii'. In abutilon, the vertical central stem influences the growth pattern of the side shoots, which are short near the top or apex of the stem and gradually become longer toward the bottom of the stem to produce a conical form. This growth pattern is called apical dominance. To form a denser cone, prune the side shoots to encourage their branching. Plants pruned into geometric forms like this are used the same way as plants that are naturally geometric or architectural. They make good container plants on both sides of your front door or in formal gardens. Place them at the four corners where two pathways intersect.

The excitement of tropical plants comes from the patterns produced by the colors, textures, and forms of both foliage and flowers. Harmonious combinations and contrasts make the exotic garden sing. When you've learned how to make all the components of your composition compatible, you've learned how to create plant combinations. Now it's time to put these plants into borders and beds.

Left: The stiff architectural outlines of *Dracaena marginata* 'Tricolor' (left), *Yucca elephantipes* (lower right), and the golden snakeplant, *Sansevieria trifasciata* 'Laurentii' (middle right), are accentuated by their contrast with more flexible forms around them. A golden *Plectranthus* trails beneath the bench as a ground cover. Nearby, the weak-stemmed and vinelike *Allamanda cathartica* is attached to the upright supports.

Right: The limp stems of wandering jew, *Tradescantia zebrina*, quickly mat into a horizontal groundcover, whereas the stems of the oyster plant, *Tradescantia spathacea* (right), are stiff and upright.

3

Tropical Borders

*I*n most people's minds borders go hand in hand with hardy perennials, as English gardens have dictated for decades. But there's no rule that restricts border plantings to hardy species. Tropical plants can be arranged within them each spring to form summer scenes that are just as attractive as an English-style perennial border.

Borders are planting spaces, usually long and rectangular, that are viewed from one side; they have a front and a rear that are generally planted with short and tall plants, respectively. Borders follow or "border" something, like the foundation of a house, a patio, a pool, or a fence. Commonly, they border driveways or walkways, edge lawns, and mark the boundary of a property. Borders may stand singly or be part of a balanced pair. When the topography of a site is rough and irregular, like a hillside

with rocky outcrops, an informal variation that combines soft curves with the elements of nature is more appropriate than a strict rectangle. Wherever borders are positioned on the home property, a well-designed border has plants within it arranged according to their color, texture, and form.

Any strip of soil that is dug and planted to be viewed from one side may be considered to be a border, but the best borders are those that are part of a greater garden design. I prefer tropical borders not to border the fringe of the property but to be in the center of it, closely related to the house and within the framework of a traditional enclosed and symmetric garden. In this garden design style, a pair of borders flank a central pathway that radiates from the house and connects the borders to the house. This way, the borders are clearly visible from your home and become part of it. Around their rear, an enclosure, either a wall, fence, or hedge, creates an outdoor garden room, *an exotic garden*, a complete and framed composition (as shown at right).

Tropical Borders as Part of an Enclosed Garden

As part of a garden that is enclosed on four sides by walls, fences, or hedges, borders are a great place to grow and display tropical plants outside of the tropics. Enclosures like these will shield border plants from winds that aren't tropical but are often too cool and too dry. Large, coarse-textured leaves are less likely to be torn. Enclosures also trap moisture within the space to create humidity levels that are closer to those in Florida or the Caribbean. And enclosures define and limit the maintenance, making the workload clear and manageable.

When exotic tropicals are isolated in an enclosed garden room they are segregated from most everyday winter-hardy plants. Although they can be handsomely combined with many hardy plants (as at Montrose Gardens), they are often too disparate; hibiscus and bananas are jarring next to azaleas and woodland

Enclosed Borders Create a Tropical Garden Room

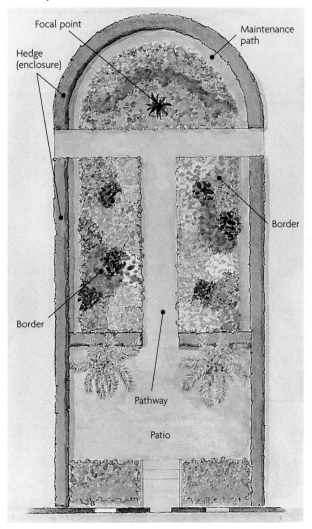

Focal point

Maintenance path

Hedge (enclosure)

Border

Border

Pathway

Patio

rhododendrons. Their geographic and ecological origins on the planet are too distant.

When you enter an enclosed garden space where the borders are planted solely with tropical plants (and you're *not* in the tropics), the impact is powerful. Wow! Bananas, palm trees, and bougainvillea vines. Where am I? Is this Long Island or the Virgin Islands? Within this private garden the plants dictate the theme: exotic, faraway places where the colors are as

Modeled on the Indian paradise garden, the enclosed tropical garden at SUNY Farmingdale has a pool of water at its center. A pair of borders flank a bluestone walkway.

Border

Bench

Maintenance path

Hedge

Pool

Walkway

hot as the day and the scent sits in the still and sultry atmosphere. Here, the jungle is tamed; order and management rule. This enclosed garden is your tropical world, a retreat reminiscent of a flight to the Caribbean, a surprise garden different from any other.

Enclosed exotic gardens are traditional, mimicking the quartered or "chahar bagh" paradise garden, such as the Taj Mahal garden, of 16th- and 17th-century Mughal India. In these gardens, massed plantings of exotic fruit trees—pomegranates, citrus, date palms, and Abyssinian bananas—in four quadrants bordered perpendicular walks or water channels. Jasmine, oleander, and pandanus scented the air. At the intersection of major walkways were pools of water, where the sacred lotus grew.

An enclosed exotic garden doesn't need to have the historic proportions of the Taj Mahal garden. When the scale is reduced to a backyard, these garden spaces become intimate. While the space is geometric and the borders within it are symmetric, the plants can be arranged informally, more like a cottage garden in the tropics, and be very personal.

The Indian paradise garden is a model for the tropical garden at the State University of New York at Farmingdale, New York, where I teach ornamental horticulture. In a rectangular space, a balanced pair of borders is enclosed by a yew hedge planted over 50 years ago (see the photo and plan on the facing page). A rectangular pool in its center calls to mind a Mughal garden. Within the borders some plants are arranged symmetrically, like architectural yuccas, bold bananas, and unique palms. The remaining plants are arranged asymmetrically, as in a cottage garden, but are organized by their color, texture, and form (see the planting plan on p. 53).

Constructing Enclosed Borders

If your home sits on level ground and has a symmetric and classic facade, enclosed tropical borders that mimic its symmetry are the best garden design. And they're easy to create. First, determine where you want the primary garden view to be from: from the center doorway, a secondary entrance (kitchen or rear), a porch, a terrace, or an important window. Then, position a central sight line, called the primary axis, to radiate from that point into the proposed garden site. This line will become the center pathway. Along both sides of the center pathway lay down borders, from about 5 ft. to 12 ft. wide (whatever width is best for the overall garden scheme), where you'll arrange and plant tropicals. A secondary axis can bisect the center pathway at its middle to create four quadrants, as in the Mughal garden.

Terminate the primary axis with a focal point where you want the garden to end. The focal point should be a special object or plant that stops the view. It's the garden's crescendo that everything else leads to. Good candidates for this honor include vases and other containers (see the photo on p. 46), statues, sundials, birdbaths, fountains or pools, furniture, gazebos, or a summerhouse. If a secondary axis is used, one of these focal points can be positioned where the two axes bisect. The pathways then widen around the object.

After the primary and secondary axes are positioned, enclose the garden space with a fence, wall, hedge, or unpruned shrubbery (as if you're framing a picture) to create an outdoor garden room. Leave an unplanted space approximately 2 ft. wide between the rear of the border and the enclosure so that air can circu-

When placed upon a pedestal, a densely planted cast-iron vase makes a special focal point. This vase contains the architectural New Zealand flax (*Phormium tenax* 'Purpureum') and cascading spider plants (*Chlorophytum comosum* 'Vittatum').

late freely around the plants. This space also functions as a rear maintenance path. (For tips on sizing the garden, see the facing page.)

Since right angles dominate this garden style, it's easy to test the proposed design to be certain you'll be happy with it before you begin construction. Mark the garden where it will go on your property with stakes and string or a brightly colored plastic ribbon. The messiest phases of construction are installation of a permanent enclosure and a center pathway, so construct them first. If you prepare soil before they are finished, it will only get trampled.

Creating the enclosure

There are almost as many kinds of enclosures as there are kinds of plants, and the one you choose will determine the enclosure's longevity and cost. Enclosures can be permanent and last for generations or be temporary and enclose a garden for a single season. The material and style of a permanent enclosure should be harmonious with the construction material and style of the house. Walls, either stone or brick, are as durable as the house itself and can sometimes require a mortgage for their financing.

Fences fit better into smaller budgets and smaller sites. Their narrow width takes less space than a wall or hedge. Temporary snow fences are cheap and easy to install and can be both effective and attractive. Attach them firmly to strong corner posts and paint them to coordinate or contrast with the garden color. Roll on a new paint color each spring as you change the garden theme. Anything goes!

Hedges, either permanent or temporary, require more labor. Certain varieties of yew, holly, and arborvitae make good permanent

Sizing the Garden

The best overall size for your outdoor garden room is one where the width and length reflect a set of numbers in the mathematical Fibonacci series, like 3 and 5, 5 and 8, 8 and 13, 13 and 21, or 21 and 34. A number in the Fibonacci series (0, 1, 1, 2, 3, 5, 8, 13, 21, 34, 55, 89...) is formed by the addition of the previous two numbers. In this series the proportion of one number to its subsequent number is approximately 1:1.618, which is commonly known as the golden mean or golden section. It is the proportion the ancient Greeks considered to be "ideal." Architects have traditionally used it to create a rectangle that is most pleasing to the human eye. Look around you to see how many "classic" manufactured objects use this proportion, such as a 3-in. by 5-in. index card. Forms in nature also reflect this ideal. It is often found in the arrangement of component parts of an organism, as in the spiral of seeds within a sunflower or in the spiral of bracts on a cone of a Norway spruce.

You can use the golden mean to determine the boundary size of your exotic garden simply by multiplying the width by 1.618 to determine the length. To find the width of the enclosed space, add together the widths of the borders, their rear maintenance paths, and the center pathway. For example, if both borders are each 6 ft. wide, the mainte-

nance paths are each 1 ft. wide, and the center pathway is 4 ft. wide, the total width is 18 ft. Multiply 18 ft. by 1.618, to get the length, 29.124 ft., and round it to a close digit, either 29 or 30. To me,

18 ft. by 30 ft. seems like a good size for the enclosed garden. Alternatively, choose two adjacent numbers within the Fibonacci series, like 21 and 34, to be the width and length of the enclosure.

Proportion of Width to Length in a Golden-Mean Rectangle

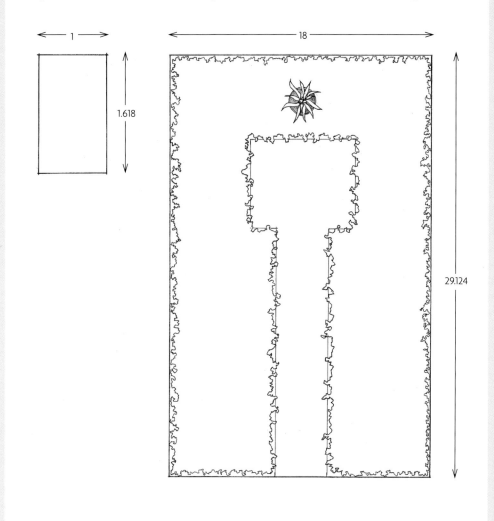

At **SUNY Farmingdale**, an old yew hedge encloses the tropical garden. *Ensete ventricosum* 'Maurelii' and *Musa acuminata* 'Dwarf Cavendish' (at right) are planted into the garden first in May.

hedges when pruned. *Ilex* 'Blue Girl', *Thuja occidentalis* 'Nigra', and varieties of yew are among the neatest and easiest to prune and maintain. They provide a restful green background for the riotous tropical plants.

Seasonal hedges of tropical plants, those replaced each year, give you the freedom to test your design before you commit to something permanent. And they don't break a budget. The annual summer cypress, *Bassia scoparia* 'Trichophylla' (syn. *Kochia trichophylla*), is quick to produce a very compact, conical yewlike form. In good soil the plant grows 3 ft. to 5 ft. tall and shears well. Linear leaves, 2 in. to 3 in. long, become a deep red-bronze in autumn and give rise to the other common name, burning bush (not to be confused with the shrub burning bush, *Euonymus alatus*, which is sometimes also grown as a hedge). The dead skeleton of the summer cypress provides form for some of the winter until crushed by heavy snow. Sow the seeds in mid-April to plant outside in mid-May or sow seeds directly outdoors on May 1. Plants should stand about 18 in. apart.

The deep reddish-bronze color of the 3-in. to 4-in. lobed leaves of the tropical *Hibiscus acetosella* 'Red Shield' lasts until frost. When used as a hedge, the leaves provide a background

color that enhances all other plants. In May, space and plant *Hibiscus acetosella* 'Red Shield' in prepared soil in sun about 18 in. to 24 in. apart. Stem cuttings root easily in spring or can be purchased inexpensively at many garden centers. Provide each plant with a strong center support, to which you'll tie the branches. Fertilize to encourage tall growth, and then pinch to thicken branching. Two-year-old plants make the thickest hedge.

Tall stately canna varieties, reaching 6 ft. or more, may be the easiest and best seasonal hedge choice. Large leaves, about 18 in. long and 6 in. wide in shades of green or bronze (some striped like a zebra), are densely arranged around strong, upright stems to shield all views. They are resistant to the force of wind and rarely rip or shred. Plants are tough and grow quickly. Plant rhizomes directly into prepared soil in early May or, for a faster start, begin them indoors in early April for planting outside in mid-May. Stagger them down the row about 18 in. apart. For a tall hedge, be sure to select one of the tall cultivars, such as *Canna* 'Ambassador'. As a bonus, your hedge will bloom with hot exotic colors all summer long.

Creating the pathways

To enter your tropical world, you need a center pathway. It is the link between the house and the garden, and it also divides the space in half. Center or primary pathways are simply formed by widening the center sight line, that is, the primary axis. The pathway should be wide enough for a couple to walk arm in arm, at least 4 ft. to 6 ft. wide, and can be composed of any kind of material. I like simple paths of crushed gravel (the size of a pea) or weathered brick. The walkway in the Tropical Garden at Farmingdale, which preexisted the garden, is bluestone. It requires less maintenance than gravel or brick but costs more. A mowed and

When *Hibiscus acetosella* 'Red Shield' is trained into a seasonal hedge, the burgundy-colored leaves provide a background color that enhances all other plants.

edged turf walk is the least expensive and can look good, but the dew will wet your feet during morning strolls and the grass needs to be kept from encroaching into the border.

To install a path, first mark the walkway with stakes and string. Make sure the width of the path remains consistent along its entire length. Remove any existing turf, then excavate 6 in. deep (add the removed soil to the planting spaces), grade, and level the ground. To confine the paving material within the walkway, edge the space with brick, Belgian block, wood (redwood or cedar to resist rot), or steel edging.

For a gravel walkway, layer 3 in. of drainage material between the edges. On top of the drainage layer, add a 3-in. pea-gravel mixture (about 70% gravel and 30% loam), as shown in the drawing at left. Loam helps the gravel to pack tightly. Using an iron rake, grade the gravel mixture to be slightly higher in the walkway's center than along its margin. Compact

Cross Section of Walk

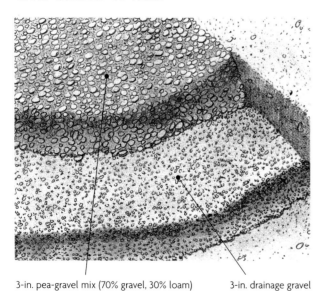

3-in. pea-gravel mix (70% gravel, 30% loam)　　　3-in. drainage gravel

the gravel with a sod tamper or roller. Maintain gravel walkways with a fan rake and remove weeds as they germinate. Pre-emergent herbicides help minimize this task.

Brick provides a traditional surface in an array of warm earthy tones. When installed in sand, different patterns, called bonds, give a natural look at minimum cost. Some, like the running bond and basket weave, are easier for a less-skilled bricklayer to install than others, such as the herringbone. To lay a brick walkway, begin as for a gravel one. Excavate to 6 in., grade, level the ground, and position the edges. Then put in a perfectly level sand base of about 3 in. and carefully arrange the brick in your chosen pattern. Fill the spaces between the bricks with more sand. I find this gives the garden path an antique, weathered look, which I prefer to brick set in concrete. Brick laid in sand will move as the frozen winter soil moves, so rework the brick as needed in spring.

The paths at the Andromeda Botanic Garden in Barbados, first made by its creator the late Iris Bannochie, are composed of rectangular and circular concrete slabs. In each slab Iris embedded a leaf of a philodendron, palm, or any other plant with a unique tropical silhouette (see the photo at right). The slab retains the image like the celebrity footprints in front of Grauman's Chinese Theater in Hollywood. When the slabs are used for a path, the tunnel of tropical foliage is not only overhead but also underfoot.

Preparing the soil

There's no escaping it. For best plant growth, all new borders, no matter what is to be planted within them, need their soil prepared two spades deep (about 16 in.). This allows plant roots to penetrate deeply and quickly into the earth where the soil remains moist longer than on the soil surface; therefore, growth is better.

If there's turf where your borders are to go, as there was on our borders, remove it. Begin the project in late summer or early autumn so the soil has time to settle before spring planting. My landscape-gardening students removed the turf for our tropical garden with a rented sod cutter in less than an hour; but for small borders it may be easier to sever the grass from its root system with a sharp spade, mattock, or grape hoe. Then begin soil preparation. Dig the top 8 in. of soil with a spade and stockpile it onto a sheet of burlap laid next to the border. Fork the remaining subsoil an additional

When concrete is poured into a mold with tropical leaves at its base, a unique pathway material with a tropical flavor is created. This pathway is in the Andromeda Botanic Gardens, Barbados.

Cross Section of Soil Preparation

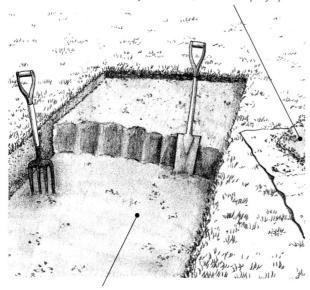

Stockpile the top layer of soil beside the border (return after bottom layer is worked, then work top layer).

Work the bottom layer in place (fork with organic matter, superphosphate, 5-10-5).

8 in. deep. Add and mix 3 in. to 6 in. of organic matter to the lower soil level. We use steam-pasteurized leaf mold, but any sterilized compost (proper composting produces a sterile product), composted manure, or peat moss is good.

The next stage is like making a cake. Add superphosphate and 5-10-5 (nitrogen-phosphorus-potassium) fertilizer and mix at the rate of 5 lb. per 100 sq. ft. Adjust the pH to approximately 6.5 by incorporating either limestone or aluminum sulfate. Replace the top 8-in. soil layer and add the same organic matter and fertilizer amendments. Finally, apply the icing and grade the border with a 24-in. aluminum grading rake or a 12-in. iron rake.

If you don't happen to have a class of young, strong, and eager landscape-gardening students at hand, you can simplify my procedure by using a rototiller. This is acceptable for soil that has previously been worked and is soft. Rototill half the total organic matter and fertilizer recommendations into the top 8 in. of soil.

Designing Tropical Borders

After the borders are positioned and prepared, they are ready to be designed. Once you become familiar with tropical plants and how they respond to temperate conditions, you'll find they are easier to design with than winter-hardy perennials. Since most tropical plants produce flowers continually, and much of the exotic garden effect is from foliage, the problem of bloom sequence that you encounter in a traditional perennial border isn't a concern in a tropical border.

Establishing a color theme

First, establish a color theme, following the guidelines presented in chapter 2. Then, choose plants to match it. Consult the glossary and the section on variegated plants in this chapter (pp. 59–63) to decide what plants you would most like to grow; then, if possible, study them in a botanic garden conservatory, greenhouse, or garden center.

The color theme for my 1997 tropical garden at SUNY Farmingdale varied from red through orange and warm salmon-pink to yellow—hot colors—to create a hot tropical mood. In the northwest quadrant, red flowers, *Hibiscus rosa-sinensis* and *Pentas lanceolata* among them, were combined with bronze-foliage plants like *Pseuderanthemum atropurpureum* and *Ricinus*

In the northwest quadrant of SUNY Farmingdale's tropical garden, red flowers—*Canna* 'Ambassador', *Acalypha hispida*, *Pentas lanceolata*, and *Salvia splendens*—combine with purplish-foliaged *Tradescantia pallida* 'Purple Heart', *Strobilanthes dyerianus*, *Colocasia* 'Fontanesii', and *Colocasia* 'Illustris'.

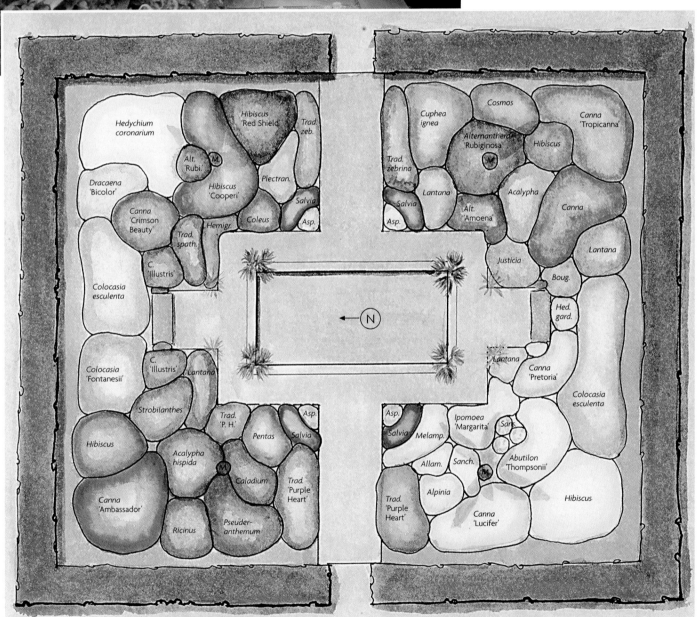

Hedychium coronarium

Hibiscus 'Red Shield'

Trad. zeb.

Alt. 'Rubi.'

M

Dracaena 'Bicolor'

Plectran.

Hibiscus 'Cooperi'

Salvia

Canna 'Crimson Beauty'

Coleus

Asp.

Hemigr.

Trad. spath.

C. 'Illustris'

Colocasia esculenta

Cuphea ignea

Cosmos

Canna 'Tropicanna'

Alternanthera 'Rubiginosa'

M

Hibiscus

Trad. zebrina

Lantana

Acalypha

Salvia

Alt. 'Amoena'

Canna

Asp.

Lantana

Justicia

Boug.

Hed. gard.

N

Colocasia 'Fontanesii'

C. 'Illustris'

Lantana

Strobilanthes

Trad. 'P. H.'

Asp.

Pentas

Salvia

Hibiscus

Acalypha hispida

M

Caladium

Trad. 'Purple Heart'

Canna 'Ambassador'

Ricinus

Pseuder- anthemum

Lantana

Canna 'Pretoria'

Colocasia esculenta

Asp.

Salvia

Melamp.

Ipomoea 'Margarita'

Sars.

Allam.

Sanch.

Abutilon 'Thompsonii'

M

Trad. 'Purple Heart'

Alpinia

Canna 'Lucifer'

Hibiscus

In the northeast quadrant, white variegated foliage—*Hibiscus rosa-sinensis* 'Cooperi' (center) and *Dracaena marginata* 'Bicolor'—combines with red flowers (*Canna* 'Crimson Beauty') and purplish foliage (*Tradescantia spathacea*).

In the southwest quadrant, golden foliage, golden variegation—*Sanchezia speciosa* (left) and *Alpinia zerumbet* 'Variegata' (right)—and golden flowers predominate.

In the southeast quadrant, orange and warm salmon pink create the theme: *Acalypha wilkesiana* 'Macrophylla' (center), *Alternanthera ficoidea* 'Amoena', and *Justicia brandegeana* (lower right). Appropriately hued canna, coleus, and hibiscus join in the display.

communis 'Carmencita', purple-foliage plants like *Tradescantia pallida* 'Purple Heart' and *Strobilanthes dyerianthus*, and the blackish *Colocasia esculenta* 'Illustris'. Red steps forward, bronze steps back. *Canna* 'Ambassador' brought both red flowers and bronze foliage into the picture.

In the northeast quadrant, red flowers and bronze foliage mix with white variegated foliage plants: *Ficus elastica* 'Variegata Robusta', *Dracaena marginata* 'Bicolor', and *Hibiscus rosa-sinensis* 'Cooperi'. As if that wasn't variegated enough, I underplanted the leggy *Dracaena marginata* 'Bicolor' with the white-striped wandering jew, *Tradescantia fluminensis* 'Albovittata'.

Diagonally opposite in the southwest quadrant, the white variegation is balanced with yellow variegated foliage plants: *Canna* 'Pretoria', *Abutilon pictum* 'Thompsonii', *Sansevieria trifa-*

sciata 'Laurentii', *Sanchezia speciosa*, and *Alpinia zerumbet* 'Variegata'. All are similar in color yet different in leaf size and form. I combined them with yellow flowers to form a mostly monochromatic arrangement.

Between the two kinds of variegation, in the southeast quadrant, orange and salmon-pink flowers and foliage are dominant. Orange-flowered *Cosmos sulphureus*, *Cuphea ignea*, and *Lantana camara* blend with salmon-pink-flowered *Hibiscus rosa-sinensis* and the shrimp plant (*Justicia brandegeana*). They drift harmoniously among the warm pink leaves of *Alternanthera ficoidea* 'Amoena' and three cultivars of *Acalypha wilkesiana*. This design was different from the arrangement I'd tried the previous year—it's always good to use last year's learned experience to improve next year's garden.

Arranging the plants

Once you've established a theme and selected the plants that will help you achieve it, you're ready to draw your border on a piece of graph paper. Choose a scale, such as 1 in. equals 1 ft. or 1 in. equals 4 ft., and then start with one border at a time. Divide borders less than 6 ft. wide in half lengthwise to form a foreground and a rear. Borders wider than 6 ft. can accommodate more plants, so divide them into thirds to form a foreground, middle, and rear. Generally, short plants, 3 ft. and under, will go into the foreground, taller plants into the middle and rear. It's okay to break this rule occasionally and place tall plants in the front for surprise. Sort your plant list by height into categories of short (less than 3 ft.), medium (between 3 ft. and 5 ft.), and tall (greater than 5 ft.). Bear in mind that a larger number of shorter plants will fit into the foreground than kinds of taller plants will fit into the rear.

Subsort each height list into plant combinations, that is, groups of plants you want to see growing next to each other. Use the design principles of color, texture, and form to create them (see chapter 2). In general, the best plant combinations occur when plants of similar flower and leaf colors (analogous colors) but of opposing textures and plant forms are positioned side by side. Arrange the combinations artistically on the graph paper in pleasing "drifts"—loosely flowing masses of a single kind of plant, similar to those in the designs in the drawing at right and on p. 53. Position architectural plants as accent and corner plants first. In tropical borders, architectural plants break the rules of a traditional border: They reign and outnumber accents used in a standard perennial border. It's part of the nature of tropical plants. They can't stop their flamboyance!

Arranging Plants in a Border

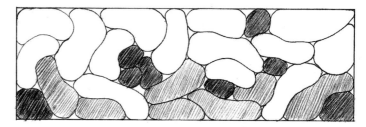

KEY

Architectural plants

Shorter, foreground plants

Taller, rear plants

The best combinations occur when plants of similar flower and leaf colors, but of opposing textures and plant forms, are positioned side by side, like *Dracaena marginata* 'Tricolor' and *Acalypha wilkesiana* 'Marginata'.

Design the foreground next, and then place middle and rear plants into their drifts. Remember to keep in mind the mature size of plants and don't overcrowd at this stage; but be certain all soil will be hidden by midsummer.

Once you've completed the design of the first border you can design its mate on the opposite side of the center pathway. The easiest way to design a pair of borders is to make them mirror images of each other. This will create an orderly balance. However, you can also achieve balance without mirror-image symmetry, a bit more informally, and with greater interest. Different plants of similar color, texture, and form are opposite one another, achieving a sense of balance but not identical balance. This arrangement harmoniously introduces the largest number of plant varieties without creating a chaotic collection.

When the planting plan is complete, the soil is prepared, and night temperatures are above 50°F, it's time to plant. To position plants in the border as they are on the plan, I first insert bamboo stakes along the border's length, using a tape measure that correlates to the scale of the plan to guide me. For example, put stakes 4 ft. apart if the scale is 1 in. equals 4 ft., or 5 ft. apart when the scale is 1 in. equals 5 ft. I find this makes translating distances from the plan to the garden easier.

So as not to damage small plants, I position and plant large specimens and architectural plants first, followed by medium-sized plants. The smallest plants enter the soil last. If I want to make a plant appear taller than it actually is, I'll leave it in its pot on top of the soil rather than planting it directly into the border. A mat of newspaper below the pot helps keep insects from entering through the drainage hole. To hide the pot I plant fast-growing varieties, like coleus, in front of it.

An architectural *Yucca elephantipes* anchors a corner in the northwest quadrant of the 1998 garden. In the foreground, red verbena weaves through three clumps of *Caladium* 'Freida Hemple'; *Jatropha integerrima* and *Acalypha hispida* are in the middle of the border; *Canna* 'Ambassador' is in the rear.

I plant with some order, generally from left to right. However, as I'm planting, my process of design refinement begins. Maybe a plant combination that seemed effective on paper doesn't work outdoors. So I change it. Or sometimes the actual size of a plant is larger than I envisioned on paper and plants need to be spread apart, or vice versa. Plants may need to be closer, opening spaces that require additional plants. Often I'll leave an unplanned space for a treasure I know I'll find later at a nursery. My design refinement continues for several weeks—plants move around, some come out, others go in—until I feel the composition is as perfect as it will be for that season. I'll refine again next year.

Swimming-Pool Gardens

Swimming pools are often incongruous with their environment, even when designed with curving lines to look natural. When they're painted aquamarine or turquoise, their waters are more akin to those of the Caribbean Sea than a local woodland pond. So you might as well intensify this theme and repeat majesty palms down the length of the borders to resemble coconut palms on a Caribbean beach. Only then can a total harmony begin.

If you're planning a new swimming pool or whirlpool, consider a tropical scheme like the design shown below. A simple central rectangle, flanked with pathways, borders, and enclosure, is best. Terminate the axis with a bathhouse or cabana made of brightly colored canvas. Clusters of containers can increase the number of colorful tropical plants.

Swimming-Pool Garden Plan

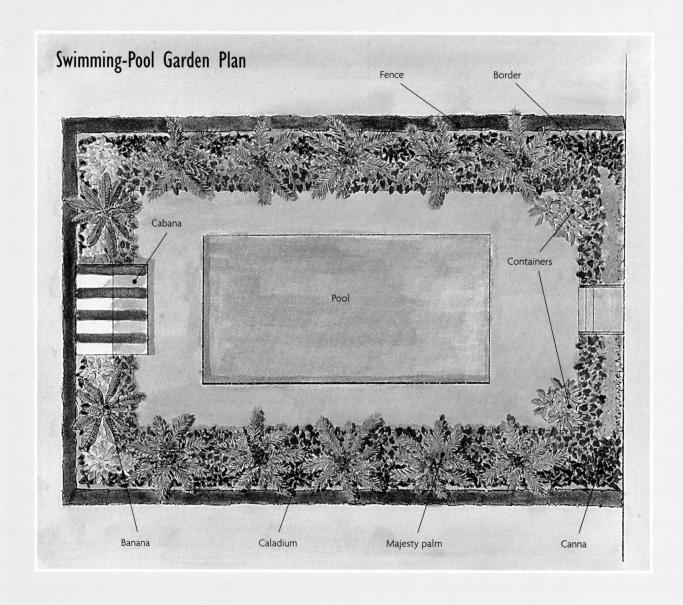

Fence

Border

Cabana

Containers

Pool

Banana

Caladium

Majesty palm

Canna

Dracaena reflexa 'Song of India', one of the best variegated houseplants, will brighten shady areas outdoors or can be acclimated to higher light levels. In both locations its growth is slow.

Variegated Plants for Tropical Borders

You can use almost any of the plants listed in the glossary in a tropical border, but I find variegated-leaved plants particularly effective, used either sparingly or lavishly. They produce a show that doesn't stop. Flowers, which can be short-lived, aren't the main act; the brilliant leaves are the stars that demand attention. Variegated plants spice up a tropical border all season long.

A variegated plant is a plant that develops patches and patterns of different colors, or absences of green pigment, in its foliage. Numerous kinds exist, both temperate and tropical. Most forms of variegation are caused by mutations within the dividing cells of the plant's shoot meristem, that is, its growing point. The green chloroplast, where photosynthesis occurs, is absent or dysfunctional and is sometimes replaced with yellow carotene or red anthocyanin pigments. Parts of the leaf then appear yellow or red. When they are not present cells appear white. Neighboring green tissues need to nourish the nonphotosynthetic tissues. Nature is harsh on mutant plants, and they are rare in the wild. They require the constant coddling of cultivation if they are to survive, which is part of their appeal.

The simplest variegated leaf has a margin without green chlorophyll that is either white or yellow. Old terms for such leaves are "Albo-Marginata" or "Aureo-Marginata," respectively. Leaf centers also lose their chlorophyll and

Left: *Alpinia zerumbet* 'Variegata' (at left) has the most ornamental foliage of the ginger relatives and is sold as a houseplant.

Below: Many variegated cultivars of *Acalypha wilkesiana* exist. In *Acalypha wilkesiana* 'Macrophylla', leaf colors change from a blush of peach to burgundy as they mature.

are white or yellow. Some monocots, plants with leaf veins arranged parallel to each other, have leaves striped white or yellow. Dicots, plants with leaf veins arranged like a net, are often speckled.

Variegated foliage provides a rich color palette for the tropical border. The "green" portion of the leaf may be gray-green, yellow-green, or blue-green. The variegated portion offers a spectrum of white, cream, yellow, gold, pink, red, burgundy, and purple—sometimes all mixed together into a veritable Joseph's coat.

I like to combine variegated plants of certain leaf colors with plants that have a similar flower color, like the snowbush (*Breynia nivosa* 'Roseapicta') and the Egyptian star (*Pentas lanceolata*). The leaves of the snowbush are striped in reddish-pink, burgundy, and white; the flowers of the Egyptian star are carmine red.

Similarly, golden variegated plants with contrasting textures, like *Canna* 'Pretoria', *Alpinia zerumbet* 'Variegata', *Sanchezia*, and *Abutilon pictum* 'Thompsonii', glisten when combined with sunny-yellow flowering plants like *Allamanda cathartica, Allamanda schottii,* and yellow *Lantana* cultivars. Bring the architectural golden snake plant (*Sansevieria trifasciata* 'Laurentii') into the composition to contrast both texture and form but still keep the colors similar.

Leaves of *Abutilon pictum* 'Thompsonii' are sporadically speckled yellow. Here, the variegation is caused by the Abutilon Mosaic Virus and yields a brilliant, golden leaf. Long-stalked, three- to five-lobed leaves resemble those of a swamp maple and contribute to its common name, flowering maple or parlor maple. However, their alternate arrangement on the stem should prevent any confusion with true maples of the genus *Acer,* which have their leaves arranged opposite each other.

Along with the golden variegation of *Abutilon pictum* 'Thompsonii' you also get a floral bonus. Flowers are similar in shape to those of its rela-

tives hollyhock and hibiscus, all members of the plant family Malvaceae, but are pendulous and shrimp-orange in color. Bell-like flowers, 1 in. to 2 in. long, dangle from the leaf axils. They are produced most freely in late summer and autumn when days begin to shorten.

Throughout the tropical world, *Manihot esculenta,* or cassava, is grown for its edible and tasty root tuber, which provides strength and energy. From baseball-bat-like roots, a multitude of chips, flours, and juices are produced, none of which are why I grow cassava. I love the leaves of the variegated sport, which blend nicely with the other golden variegated plants. Neat, deeply lobed, five-fingered leaf blades, about 3 in. to 6 in. long, have green margins and golden yellow centers that fade to cream. They spiral around 3-ft. to 5-ft. stems, attached by bright red petioles. Stems branch as they grow tall to become a handsome accent plant.

Variegated cassava, *Manihot esculenta* 'Variegata', may be fussy to overwinter, but once planted outdoors in sunshine and a rich soil it flourishes when temperatures get hot.

Abutilon pictum 'Thompsonii' has been grown in gardens for over a century.

Speckled, Splotched, and Striped Acanths

If you're mad for variegation, you must become familiar with the acanths, spectacular plants within the Acanthaceae family. Leaves on these shrubby plants are opposite, which adds a stiff and coarse quality that needs no introduction. Terminal spikes of small flowers are pleasant, but not spectacular like the leaves, where almost every color can be found. These tropical plants grow fast when temperatures rise above 60°F, and they suffer at temperatures below 55°F.

Three acanths, *Sanchezia speciosa*, *Pseuderanthemum atropurpureum*, and *Graptophyllum pictum*, are favorites; my tropical garden can't be without them. The elliptic leaves of *Sanchezia* are the largest, 6 in. to 12 in. long. Golden bands border the midrib and main veins. The variegation in *Pseuderanthemum* is the most variable. Colors can range from purple, bronze, red to rose, and on another species, *Pseuderanthemum reticulatum*, from gold, yellow, cream to chartreuse. *Gratophyllum pictum* is the only species with a common name, the caricature plant. Its leaves have a center heart of creamy yellow or rose pink that may remind you of some distorted facial caricature. Some cultivars are gold, whereas others are burgundy.

Sanchezia speciosa is one of the easiest and most satisfying variegated plants to grow.

The nomenclature of *Graptohyllum* (left) and *Pseuderanthemum* (right) is baffling, but their variegation is stunning and the plants grow easily in full sun.

Position *Costus speciosus* 'Variegatus' in borders where you can easily touch the soft, velvety leaf undersurface.

Spider plants, *Chlorophytum comosum* 'Vittatum', may be common houseplants, but they are exotic in a tropical border, bed, or container. Use them generously. Here, a spider plant is combined with *Plectranthus madagascariensis* 'Variegated Mintleaf' for textural contrast.

Try red or white variegation combinations in a border as well, like *Acalypha wilkesiana*, *Hibiscus rosa-sinensis* 'Cooperi', and the crepe ginger (*Costus speciosus* 'Variegatus'). Shiny, coppery-red leaves of *Acalypha wilkesiana* are large (5 in. to 8 in. long) and change colors as they grow. *Hibiscus rosa-sinensis* 'Cooperi' is a variegated form of the shrubby red-flowered patio hibiscus. Leaf coloration is intensified by high sunlight, which sparkles like sunshine dancing on water, but plants survive lower light levels as well. Young stems and bases of irregularly toothed leaves become tones of carmine-red. Splendid, scarlet blossoms, 6 in. wide, are vivid, albeit sometimes shy to appear.

Plant *Costus speciosus* 'Variegatus' outdoors in warm, moist organic loam in light shade. The crepe ginger has zebralike foliage. Its rootlike rhizome isn't thick and aromatic like the true ginger (*Zingiber officinalis*), which is used to flavor food. Young reddish stems, 4 ft. to 6 ft. tall, spiral upward from the rhizome to look like a giant strand of DNA. Green and white oval leaves adhere to the stems like steps on a spiral staircase. On strong plants, leaves

are near 10 in. long and 3 in. wide, with soft, velvety undersides that cry out to be touched. At maturity, a cone-like spike of reddish bracts terminates the stem. Between the bracts, large, crepe-white flowers emerge to resemble jewels in a crown. Each lasts only one day, but a procession of blossoms dazzles the coronet for several weeks.

You don't need to search for the rarest plants to get the best variegation. Simply plant your variegated spider plants outdoors in the blazing sun or in dappled shade. Drift spiders in the foreground of a tropical border, outline a tropical bed (chapter 4) with them, or plant them to cascade over the edge of a container (chapter 5). They'll even survive a light frost. You may think of spider plants as common and easy to grow, but when they are planted outdoors creatively, their great color, texture, and form become unique.

4

Tropical Beds

Tropical lawn beds are part of our horticultural heritage, dating from as early as 1842. They are open planting spaces that can be viewed from all sides. Usually beds are positioned within lawns, but they can also be surrounded by gravel or any other paving material. Beds vary in shape from the simplest geometric circle or square to any amorphous form. Generally they are planted with limited kinds of plants that flower lavishly in bright colors, have bold foliar textures, and strong architectural forms.

Gardenesque Beds

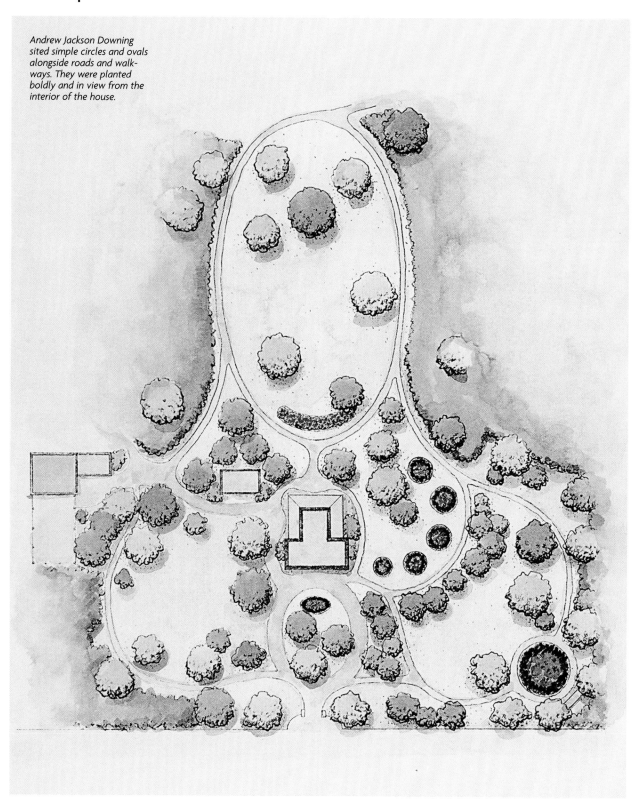

Andrew Jackson Downing sited simple circles and ovals alongside roads and walkways. They were planted boldly and in view from the interior of the house.

Victorian Tropical Lawn Beds

Lawn beds planted with mostly tropical plants were a 19th-century invention. In America, one of their earliest proponents was landscape gardener, Andrew Jackson Downing. He favored beds with massed groups of bold tropical plants like verbena, petunia, and dahlia, rather than an intermingled arrangement of flowering plants that differ in color, size, and period of bloom. Bold beds attract the eye and make a more forcible and delightful impression.

In his popular mid-19th century books and magazines, Downing praised the new tropical bedding plants that flowered nonstop from June into October and covered the soil with their brilliant color. His landscape designs show simple circles and other amoeboid shapes cut into crisply maintained lawns like cookies cut into rolled dough—what was known as the "gardenesque" style in England. Illustrations and photographs of American garden designs in the 19th century show an array of gardenesque patterns: beds scattered throughout the property, alongside its paths and roadways, opposite the front doorway, and outside windows to provide a view from inside (see the plan on the facing page).

Throughout the 19th century, gardenesque bedding shapes and styles steadily increased in complexity. Circles stretched into ovals, ellipses, teardrops, and tadpoles. Other shapes precisely imitated half-moons or stars. Stylish gardeners fluent with a compass and a ruler carved squares, pentagons, hexagons, octagons, diamonds, trapezoids, or rectangles into their well-manicured turf.

Gardenesque Bedding Shapes

Oval

Teardrop

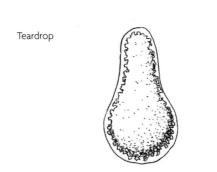

Tadpole

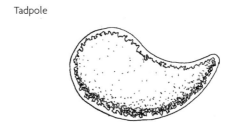

Half-moon

Star

Geometric Bedding Shapes

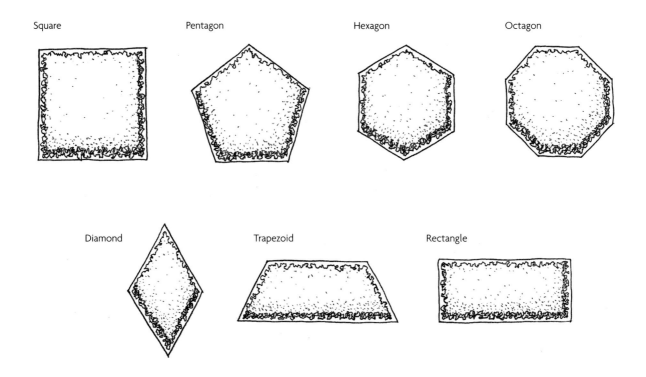

Square   Pentagon   Hexagon   Octagon

Diamond   Trapezoid   Rectangle

Within these beds, the planting design changed from year to year to include splendid new exotics and improved, or hybridized, free-flowering plants of shorter stature. In 1864, horticulturist and vice president of the Massachusetts Horticultural Society, Edward Sprague Rand Jr., used the term "bedding plants" for tender perennial plants, such as tropical plants, that need to spend the winter in the warmth of a greenhouse to survive. Lantana, cuphea, salvia, and heliotrope are examples. When they are planted outside in May, massed in beds, they bloom profusely until frost.

Landscape designer Frank Scott preferred geometric beds, like circles and hexagons, to amorphous "curlicue" or tadpole shapes for lawn beds near entrance walkways. In *Suburban Home Grounds* (1870), Scott recommended that small, 2-ft.-wide beds be filled with tropical plants of a single kind and no taller than 18 in., like the low and brightly colored foliage plants, *Alternanthera ficoidea*, *Iresine herbstii*, or coleus. They produce a neat, dense mass of solid or variegated foliage in shades of pink, red, bronze, chartreuse, or gold and do not overhang walks with unkempt growth or bloom in the spring, only to wither and then be followed by barren soil. In wide beds, Scott planted subtropical displays with large, quick-growing plants like castor bean or giant reed (*Arundo donax*) surrounded by shorter kinds in the foreground.

Geometric Beds

Frank Scott designed angular, geometric beds to be sited along straight walkways on town-size properties. They were planted with neat bedding plants that were visible from the interior of the house.

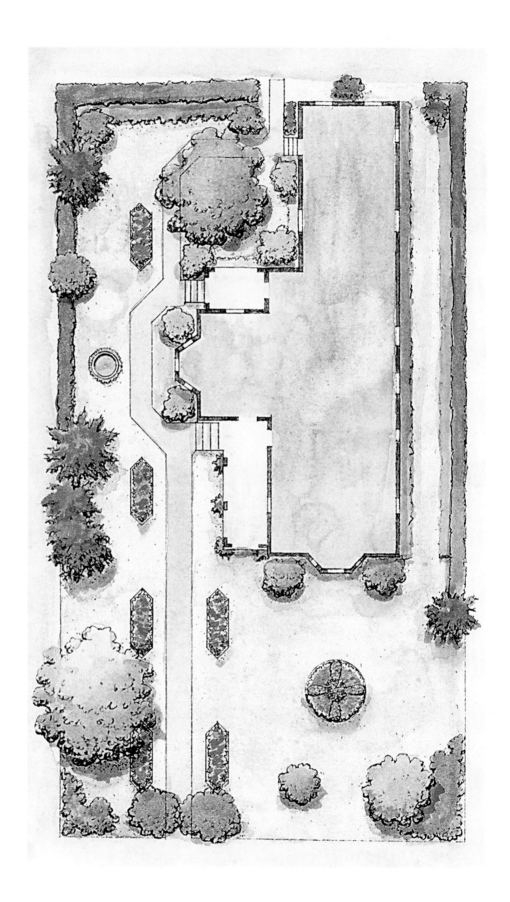

Solenostemon scutellarioides 'Saturn' is a contemporary coleus cultivar.

Today's Tropical Lawn Beds

The popular gardening periodical, *Vick's Monthly Magazine,* published by seedsman and editor James Vick, illustrated a subtropical bed in its April 1880 issue. Graceful plants native to warm climates that are easy to grow, like canna, castor beans, and elephant's ears, make this bed a simple yet sensational display.

For gardeners who want to grow tropicals picturesquely on their front lawn, beds similar to James Vick's design are an excellent model. If the lawn is in front of a Victorian house, beds like these are the quintessential embellishment. Tropical lawn beds are still seen across America in front of old court houses or civic buildings and more recently on the lawns of suburban corporate headquarters. Lawn beds can be planted with historic plants that were used during Victorian times, like canna, elephant's ears, or castor bean, or bedding varieties that have entered cultivation more recently, like the ornamental sweet potatoes 'Blackie' and 'Margarita'. Dozens more bedding plants exist today than were used a century ago. They can

BED OF SUB-TROPICAL PLANTS.

James Vick's subtropical bed, illustrated in April 1880, is composed of tropical foliage plants that sport bright color, bold texture, and statuesque form: castor bean, canna, elephant's ears, coleus, and dusty miller.

Re-created subtropical lawn beds at the historic Snug Harbor site, Staten Island, New York, are planted with plants that were common in the 19th century, like canna, pampas grass, coleus, and dusty miller.

be arranged like their Victorian predecessors with either a single species in a bed or with rings of colorful and contrasting flowers and foliage—what were known as "ribbons" in the 19th century.

Unlike a century ago, few gardeners today choose to plant in lawn beds, whether through habit, lack of information, or prejudice. Twentieth-century garden design has rejected the gardenesque style in favor of open lawns, where the only interruption to the waves of turf are the delicate shadows from fine-textured honey locust trees. Minimalists have relegated coarse-foliated cannas, castor beans, and elephant's ears to the rear of the property or dis-

missed them altogether—an unfortunate fate for plants and gardens that are such fun!

To grow tropical lawn beds, you may need to free yourself from previous conceptions of appropriate plants and styles. Nothing is wrong with crisp red salvia, especially when it is in combination with red canna like 'The President' or 'Red King Humbert'. These plants form a monochromatic scheme with contrasting textures. Palms and petunias aren't common, but they are historic and therefore deserve a prominent position, as they were given a century ago. Plants and styles you may never have considered, like circles in the lawn, can be wonderful in their proper place—which may just be your front turf.

Designing Tropical Lawn Beds

Before you start choosing tropical plants, the first step in designing your lawn bed is to determine its location and shape. Select a sunny and well-drained location. Southern, western, or eastern exposures protected from wind are best. Put beds in public view, to face the street or road.

The size of the bed should be proportional to the size of your property and home. Small lawns can accommodate one large bed, or a pair of beds, maybe 9 ft. in diameter. On larger lawns, a cluster of three or more beds, perhaps with different diameters, may fit. Plan the beds to be visible from different points around the property and from different windows in the house. If your home is irregular or asymmetric in outline—for example, a Tudor or Gothic Revival cottage or an elongated ranch from the 1950s, '60s, or '70s—irregular-shaped beds like teardrops or tadpoles will highlight its style.

Asymmetric Beds

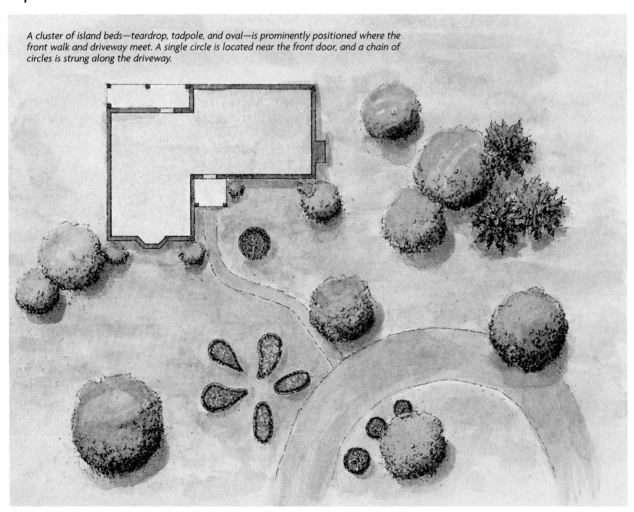

A cluster of island beds—teardrop, tadpole, and oval—is prominently positioned where the front walk and driveway meet. A single circle is located near the front door, and a chain of circles is strung along the driveway.

Cluster the beds in an asymmetric arrangement like islands in the sea. A large, single circle or a cluster of three smaller ones, asymmetrically positioned, is equally effective. However, if the facade of your house is symmetric, like those in the Georgian, Federal, Greek, Italian, or French traditions, plan a pair of symmetrically balanced beds in the front lawn on each side of the entrance, as shown below.

To fashion a bed with an irregular shape, such as kidneys, tadpoles, teardrops, or paisleys, doodle with a pencil and paper, and then sketch the winning design onto graph paper. Establish a scale like ½ in. or 1 in. equals 1 ft. To create something more geometric, use a ruler and compass. Or select a form from those illustrated on pp. 67-68. Circles were the most common Victorian form, and they are the

Symmetric Beds

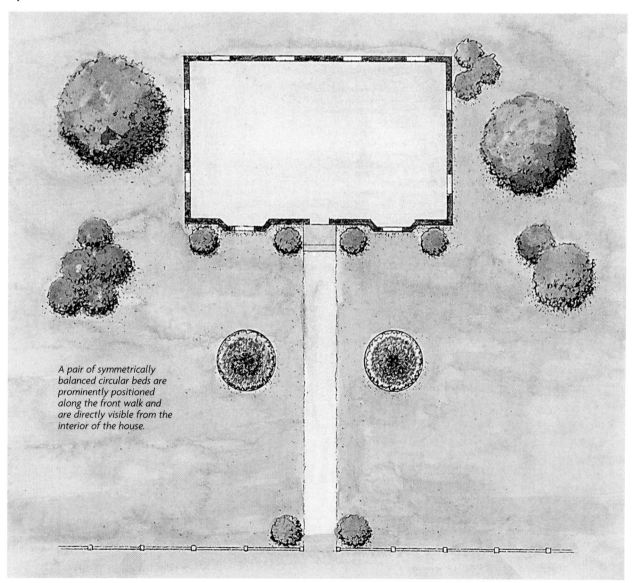

A pair of symmetrically balanced circular beds are prominently positioned along the front walk and are directly visible from the interior of the house.

easiest for first-time bedders to install and maintain. I find their simplicity usually looks better than more complicated forms, especially when accompanied with geometric architectural plants, which you'll want to include in your tropical bed.

In the 19th century, elaborate beds were designed to resemble anything from Persian carpets to kaleidoscopic patterns. They were planted with short, tight-growing plants, like sempervivum and echeveria, and were a horticultural feat. But a staff of fastidious gardeners was needed to maintain them. While I appreciate and love this horticultural craftsmanship, it's not the kind of lawn bed I'm suggesting you design. Not only are they too tedious to maintain, carpet beds like these lack the large-scale tropical plants that I love to grow, those with bold textures and statuesque forms.

Contrasting color, texture, and form

Tropical lawn beds traditionally display a strong contrast of color, texture, and form, so to design one you need to think of plants that will provide bright colors, bold textures, and architectural forms. Decide your color theme first. Don't contrast all the spectral hues in one bed, but choose just a few colors, like the primaries: red, yellow, and blue. A monochromatic design of red flowers combined with burgundy or bronze foliage will be strong and successful. Or combine one hue with its complement. Remember the rules of color: Yellow and purple complement and contrast with each other, so plant yellow and purple flowers together, like yellow lantana next to purple heliotrope or beneath a purple tibouchina standard. Or plant yellow and purple foliage plants together, such as the mottled yellow-leaved parlor maple (*Abutilon pictum* 'Thompsonii') and the purple *Tradescantia pallida* 'Purple Heart'. A similar effect can be achieved when you combine a colored foliage with a flower that is complementary in color.

Contrasting leaf textures and plant forms are critical. The distinct tropical texture provided by bananas and palms is just as appropriate in a lawn bed as in a tropical border. Each plant also brings a strong form into the composition. A single tall banana plant can become

A single specimen of sago palm (*Cycas revoluta*) makes a strong centerpiece when surrounded by a ring of red caladium. Both can be acclimated to full sun.

the center point of a 9-ft. circle; when palms are used singly as the center point, they are more in scale with a 5-ft. or 7-ft. circle. The sago palm (*Cycas revoluta*) is a dense and compact palmlike center point. Architectural species, like *Cordyline indivisa, Phormium tenax,* and *Yucca elephantipes,* are also classics for the center of a circle.

The upright stiff stems and pointed leaves of a tall canna variety will contrast nicely with the dangling and dynamic rounded leaves and mobile petioles of elephant's ears that constantly sway with the breeze. Both are large and display coarse texture, but their forms differ.

When concentric rings, or ribbons, are arranged within circular beds, tiers develop in which to

Planting Plans

Wax begonias

Red caladium

Coleus

Canna

Chinese
fan palm

*Ensete
ventricosum*

Dusty miller

A center ring of red wax begonias covers the
soil beneath a specimen of Ensete ventricosum
'Maurelii'. By summer's end it will mostly be
hidden by the next ring of red caladium and
canna. The coleus ring is rhythmically punctuated with Chinese fan palms. An outer ring of
silver dusty miller frames the composition.

*Cuphea
ignea*

Canna

Yucca

Feather
palm

Spider
plants

A feather palm, such as the inexpensive majesty
palm, is at the center of a pinwheel of Canna
'Pretoria'. Between the canna, a mass of Cuphea
ignea is punctuated by an architectural yucca.
An outer ring of variegated spider plants frames
the composition.

contrast flower and foliage colors, textures, and forms (see the drawing on the facing page). To design this kind of lawn bed all you need is a compass and graph paper. The number of rings within your circle will depend on its diameter, how many kinds of tropical plants you want to grow, and what they are. Their width can range from 1 ft. to 3 ft. or more, which is also dependent on the species planted within them; larger species require wider rings. Place the tallest plant in the circle's center, either singly or several specimens of it. Then choose plants that grade downward in height, like a pyramid, as they move outward from the center of the circle. Each ring should contrast in either color, texture, or form with the ring next to it. Usually each ring contains only a single plant variety, but sometimes two color variants of the same species can be mixed together in a ring or accent plants can move through a ring rhythmically and punctuate it.

Constructing Tropical Lawn Beds

Once the design is completed on graph paper, it's easy to scale it to your lawn. Mark the longest and widest points of an amorphous form—kidney, tadpole, teardrop, or paisley— with stakes. Then, working freehand, sketch the outline between the stakes with lime, according to your plan. (Add lime to an empty watering can, remove the breaker, and pour the lime through the spout.) Alternatively, lay a pliable garden hose on the turf between the stakes to form the bed's perimeter. Mark it with lime, and then carve the bed's outline into the turf with a sharp spade.

Prepared soil is graded into a neat, convex mound, about 10 in. higher than the surrounding turf, in this 9-ft.-diameter circle at the historic Hallockville Museum on the North Fork of Long Island, N.Y.

Dusty miller outlines the beds for tropical annuals like *Alternanthera ficoidea* and wax begonia. *Phormium tenax* 'Purpureum' marks the intersection.

Note that before you cut a bed into the lawn, it's wise to take the standard pH and soil texture tests for the proposed site. Also examine the turf to determine if noxious perennial grasslike weeds, such as nutsedge or quack grass, are present. If so, control their growth with a herbicide like Round-up or Finale (available at garden centers). If these weeds are present in the turf that surrounds the bed, try to eradicate them (otherwise, they will continue to encroach into the bed).

Constructing a circular bed requires a little simple mathematics. Hammer a peg into the turf where the circle's center is to be. Attach a cord to the peg that's half the length of the proposed circle's diameter—that is, its radius. At the end of the cord tie a pointed stake. Pull the cord tight and rotate it around the peg to form the circle. With the pointed stake, scratch the circle's circumference or outline into the turf; or mark the boundary with lime. Cut the bed's boundary with a sharp spade.

To remove the interior turf sever the grass below its crown with a spade, mattock, grape hoe, or, for large beds, a power sod cutter. Remove all excess pieces of sod from the soil. Discard, compost, or replant the sod elsewhere before turning the soil. Alternatively, kill the turf within the bed's boundary with a herbicide.

Now you can begin to enrich your soil. Since you are growing similar plants in a tropical bed as in a tropical border, you can prepare the soil in the same way. Follow the procedure to prepare border soils outlined on p. 51. The instructions seedsman Joseph Breck gave gardeners in 1851 are still sound, and obsessed Victoriaphiles may want to employ his horticultural advice. To prepare a deep, rich loam for flower beds, Breck dug trenches and added manure (peat moss wasn't commercially available in the 19th century) or carted away the poor soil and brought in good. He lightened

Cross Section of a Bed

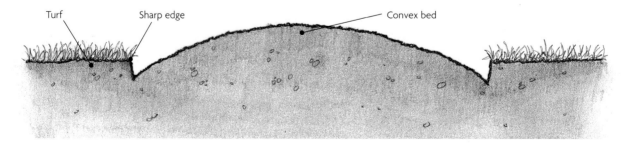

Turf   Sharp edge   Convex bed

Iresine herbstii 'Aureoreticulata' (right) and *Iresine herbstii* 'Brilliantissima' (below) were Victorian foliage favorites for massing in beds. Pinch to keep them bushy and combine with other plants from the Amaranthaceae.

heavy soil with sand. The ground was dug two spades deep, or from 12 in. to 16 in. The depth of the soil was increased by incorporating compost made from decomposed pasture grass and old rotted manure.

No matter what soil preparation method you follow, when finished the amended soil should have a light mellow texture, be rich, and abound with humus. Because of the incorporated organic matter, it will be higher than the surrounding

soil level. Grade it into a neat, convex mound, about 8 in. to 15 in. high. In addition to providing quick drainage, this mound will accentuate the bedding design. Be certain there is a sharp, clean edge between the prepared and graded soil and the surrounding turf (see the drawing on the facing page).

Once the soil has been prepared and properly graded, you can construct the rings within your circle. To construct three rings of equal width all you need is a cord, a stake hammered into the circle's center, and some lime in a watering can without its breaker. Tie a cord two-thirds the length of the radius to the center stake, and then outline a circle within the main bed. Mark it with lime. Next, reduce the cord's length to one-third of the radius; from the center stake, outline the smallest, central ring and mark it with lime. Now, position the plants on top of the soil within each ring according to your design, making certain they are spaced to grow and cover the soil by early July. Then, using a spade or a trowel, plant them into the soft earth. Regrade the soil with an iron rake or cultivator. Keep the soil neatly cultivated and weed free until the plants have grown together to form a solid ribbon. To construct five rings or ribbons of equal width, divide the cord into fifths and lime four rings.

Properly prepared beds of tropical plants can quickly form a display that commands attention. If yours didn't this year, change it for next year. It's easy, and it gives you a good excuse to experiment with new plants. What could be better than to cuddle up with seed and nursery catalogs on a snowy January day, conjure up magical and mysterious images of luxuriant tropical foliage, and rearrange a garden bed in a style reminiscent of a century ago? For most gardeners, nothing!

Plants for Tropical Beds

When selecting the best plants for a tropical bed, keep in mind the key elements of color, texture, and form. Choose plants that flower continuously, not sporadically (they go in a border). I like to see beds with bright-colored flowers, but select the flower colors you are most comfortable with. Then look at the leaves. Foliage colors should enhance the flower colors. Coarse, bold leaf textures will carry across distances better than fine textures and are showier in larger spaces. Finally, consider the overall form. Because beds are viewed from all sides, choose tall and neat architectural plants for the center of the bed, and then taper downward to low ground-covering forms near the perimeter. Avoid weak and wimpy forms when selecting plants for a bed.

Flowering favorites

Traditional "annual" plants of tropical origin like wax begonia, heliotrope, impatiens, Madagascar periwinkle, and red salvia are good bedding plants. They harmonize with plants that appear more tropical, like angel's trumpets, and they flower until frost with brilliant color. I'm partial to all the cultivated plants within the amaranth family (Amaranthaceae), like amaranthus, love-lies-bleeding, summer poinsettia (sometimes called Joseph's coat), globe amaranth (*Gomphrena*), cockscomb, and plume celosia. (Two members of the family, *Alternanthera* and *Iresine* are foliage favorites.) Most were grown in the 19th century, although contemporary hybrids often have a tighter and neater form and are available in a greater color range. All grow fast, with little effort, and are appropriate to include in a tropical lawn bed.

Ropy chenille-like tassels, usually fuchsia-pink but sometimes lime-green, drip to the ground from 4-ft.-tall plants of love-lies-bleeding

Angel's trumpets (*Brugmansia x candida*) were grown in tropical beds in Hudson Valley, New York, in the late 1840s. At the historic Mohonk Mountain House in New York State's Catskill Mountains, they are pruned into standards and annuals are bedded beneath them.

The ropy chenille-like tassels that drip to the ground from 4-ft.-tall love-lies-bleeding plants are especially handsome when used in the center of a tropical bed.

Few tropical shrubs bloom as continuously in such bright colors as *Cuphea ignea* (below) and *Lantana camara* (below right).

(*Amaranthus caudatus*). They're at their best in the center of a circle surrounded by rings of rosy-purple globe amaranth flowers, which resemble red clover, and the colorful pink and burgundy foliage of *Alternanthera* and *Iresine*. Love-lies-bleeding is a true annual plant that grows fast from seed directly sown into prepared earth in May or indoor pots in April.

Cuphea ignea and *Lantana camara*, tropical plants native to Mexico and the Caribbean islands, are often categorized with "annual" bedding plants. Currently, they are experiencing a renaissance in popularity. Both species flower continuously from May planting until frost. *Cuphea ignea*, listed as *Cuphea platycentra* in old garden books, is a sparkling little gem always in bloom. One-inch-long, narrow tubular flowers, vermilion-red with a dark ring at their tip and a white mouth, give the plant its common names cigar flower or firecracker plant. When the flower is ready to be pollinated a purple pistil emerges from the floral tube and looks like the fiery tongue of a dragon.

Hot-colored firecracker plants intensify when bedded next to *Lantana camara,* a short shrubby plant about 4 ft. tall. Numerous small, ¼-in. verbena-like flowers, in warm shades of orange and gold, congregate into a slightly domed head the size of a quarter. When grown in a sunny bed they appear all summer until frost. Flowers open yellow or pink and change to orange or scarlet. They mature into small, ½-in.-long pineapple-looking fruits.

Both cuphea and lantana grow in most soil types, and established plants are tolerant of drought. To form the forceful and delightful impression Andrew Jackson Downing envisioned, space young plants about 9 in. apart. A month after planting, pinch them so they branch and become bushy. You want them to weave together into a carpet that completely covers the soil.

Foliage favorites

Flowers aren't a required feature for a good tropical bedding plant. Foliage plants, such as coleus, dusty miller, *Alternanthera* and *Iresine,* aroids like caladium or elephant's ears, architectural plants like *Cordyline* or *Phormium,* and bananas and palms are as interesting in a lawn

Alternanthera ficoidea produces a neat, dense mass of brightly colored foliage in shades of chartreuse or bronze.

A densely planted bed of canna *(Canna x generalis* 'City of Portland') is bordered with variegated spider plants (*Chlorophytum comosum* 'Variegatum').

bed as flowering plants. Foliage plants provide the necessary textural components of the composition and also the statuesque form.

I grow the trilogy—canna, either Indian shot (*Canna indica*) or its hybrid (*Canna x generalis*), elephant's ears *(Colocasia esculenta)*, and castor bean *(Ricinus communis)*—for their foliage; the flowers of canna and the fruits of castor bean are a bonus. These plants are effective and easy to grow in lawn beds, quickly providing a tall, dramatic display.

Indian shot *(Canna indica)*

Stately canna plants support large and noble leaves, about 18 in. long and 6 in. wide. They come in tones of green, bronze, or red; some jewels, like *Canna* 'Pretoria', are striped with gold. All leaves are resistant to the force of autumn wind and rarely rip or shred. Their bases clasp 3-ft. to 6-ft.-tall stems.

In the 19th century, their flowers were pretty but not showy: Indian shot has small flowers with narrow petals. However, the 20th-century hybrid complex (*Canna x generalis*) of which Indian shot is a parent is both showy and

The large and noble heart-shaped leaves of elephant's ears look happy and are easily seen in lawn beds.

pretty. At the apex of stiff, strong stems, flowers form in warm shades of red, orange, yellow, or pink. Each is the size of a single gladiolus. Two-toned or particolored cultivars, like the red and yellow 'Lucifer', are beautiful. The stamens of some hybrids are petal-like to give an almost double flower effect.

In 19th-century America, cannas were most frequently planted in groups or densely planted in entire lawn beds for the most desirable effect. When densely planted, cannas need not be more than 1 ft. apart. But when grown to be displayed as individual plants, they require three times as much space. Canna's pointed, tapering leaves will carry the eye upward, away from the soil below.

Everyone can grow cannas; their garden culture is simple. In May, plant rhizomes or potted plants outdoors in an enriched sunny bed after the danger of frost is past and the nights are

above 55°F. Flowers begin to appear in July. After the first frost kills the foliage, dig cannas and prepare them for winter. First, cut and discard stems. Rinse soil residues from the rhizomes. Once dry, pack them in a corrugated-cardboard container with dry sphagnum, peat moss, or excelsior. Store them until spring planting in a cool basement or garage at about 50°F. Divide large rhizomes before planting in spring.

Elephant's ears (*Colocasia esculenta*)

Robust elephant's ears are grown for their large and noble heart-shaped leaves, which can grow to 4 ft. long and 3 ft. wide. Flowers are not commonly seen. When they do appear they resemble the jack-in-the-pulpit but are creamy-white. Mature plants produce stems or leaf petioles that are 4 ft. to 5 ft. long. They emerge from a thick underground root tuber that resembles a turnip and attach to the center of the leaf blade, a condition termed "peltate." This peltate condition allows light breezes to rock the smiling leaf back and forth. They look happy and create a happy garden.

Colocasia esculenta is an aroid in the same plant family as the houseplant *Philodendron*. Old garden books name it *Caladium esculentum*. Throughout the humid tropics it is a common and important root crop. West Indians know it as dasheen or eddoe, while Pacific Island peoples call the tubers taro.

It's as easy for me to grow *Colocasia esculenta* in the tropical garden at SUNY Farmingdale as it was to grow it in my garden on the Caribbean island of Barbados. This plant's culture is like that of the canna. To achieve super-large, tropical-looking leaves, enrich the soil with lots of compost or rotted manure before planting the tubers in spring.

Water the elephant's ears frequently. It's a fun job. Like a herd of circus elephants, their ears wave back and forth, grateful for the bath. Water beads on the leaf surfaces and rolls off to the soil below. Be sure enough water has penetrated through the foliar canopy down to the soil. *Colocasia esculenta* grows best in a damp, rich, mucky soil. When weather is hot and dry it's best to let water trickle for an hour or two from a hose at the plant's base to ensure deep watering.

Castor bean (*Ricinus communis*)

Castor beans are large plants with very ornamental foliage and showy fruit. In temperate climates they are herbaceous annuals, varying from 3 ft. to 15 ft. tall. However, in the tropics they are small trees reaching 30 ft. Hundreds of varieties are known, each distinguished by color, size, form, and medicinal use.

The majestic growth of castor bean gives a very tropical look. Fan-shaped palmate leaves are massive, 1 ft. to 3 ft. across, each with 5 to 12 deeply cut lobes. Colors vary from metallic grayish-green to reddish-bronze, which is always more intense in young leaves. Red-leaved cultivars like *R.* 'Sanguineus' or *R.* 'Scarlet Queen' are choice. *R.* 'Carmencita' is

The poisonous red fruits of castor beans (*Ricinus communis* 'Carmencita') are as handsome as the large, star-shaped leaves.

By the end of August, castor beans in the center of the tropical bed at the Hallockville Museum, New York, are almost 9 ft. tall. Cannas and elephant's ears encircle them.

dwarf, only 5 ft. to 6 ft., and has purple-red leaves up to 2 ft. across. All cultivars require support from a tall bamboo stake.

Lackluster petal-less flowers are borne in 1-ft. to 2-ft. clusters, staminate flowers above pistillate ones, at the top of the plant and on side stems. They are usually hidden by foliage. Female flowers mature into three-segmented, spiny-skinned fruits, about 1 in. long, that resemble a beech nut. Fruit colors range from gray to pink and scarlet. Gorgeous red ones, as on *R*. 'Carmencita', seem luminous. Since antiquity, these plants have been cultivated for the oil of the seeds within the fruit, which contains the poison ricin. The oil is used in medicine and in the arts.

Collect ripe seeds in late summer and autumn and overwinter them in an airtight jar or wrapped in aluminum foil. Start seeds indoors in late April. Lightly scratch the large beanlike seeds with a nail file; they will germinate in 12 to 15 days. Sow seeds individually, about

½ in. deep, in a peat pot to be planted outdoors in mid-May. Try not to disturb the root system. Or in early May directly sow seed in the ground where they are to grow.

Single specimens of a large castor bean can make an attractive lawn bed, but they are more effective in a group where they contrast with other ornamental leaved plants. Punctuate the center of a freshly prepared circular bed, 7 ft. to 9 ft. in diameter, with one or three plants of the tall and coarse, burgundy-foliaged and red-fruited castor bean. Ring three to seven elephant's ears around it. Their heart-shaped leaves contrast with the jagged, starlike leaf of the castor bean, which rises above the elephant's ears like an umbrella. Frame these two plants with a ring of red-leaved coleus to create a simple, monochromatic scheme, where textures and forms contrast, not colors. It is similar to our model that was illustrated in *Vick's Monthly Magazine* in April 1880.

5 *Tropical Containers*

Container gardens make it possible for anyone to grow an exotic garden, be it on a Manhattan rooftop or a suburban patio, around a swimming pool, or in front of a garage. Growing tropical plants in pots, tubs, vases, or other decorative vessels overcomes the limitations imposed by paved surfaces, poor soil, or limited soil space. Use the design rules of color, texture, and form as if the garden were in the ground. And if you don't like the arrangement, change it. It's as easy as moving furniture in your living room.

The four corners of the rectangular pool in the Tropical Garden at SUNY Farmingdale are highlighted with four pots each of the Chinese fan palm (*Livistona chinensis*).

The tropical garden of my childhood was in a clay flowerpot. A single specimen of the annual wishbone flower (*Torenia fournieri*) stood in front of our garage one summer and was moved regularly. Other flowerpots clustered into this container garden, but the purplish-blue wishbone flower stands above them in my memory. During the wet season in Barbados, *Torenia* surprised me, popping up here and there throughout Andromeda Botanic Gardens. Now it pops up in Long Island nurseries every spring, and I plant it in clients' patio pots to introduce them to tropical containers.

Siting Containers

One of the simplest way to refine your home is to place a pair of containers, exuberantly filled with exotic plants, at each side of the front entrance. The containers will define and frame the entry. Expanding the pair into a row of containers along the front walk, through repetition of their form, will help unify the entire landscape composition. You'll quickly discover that containers seasonally planted with tropical plants can embellish all gardens, whatever their style.

Containers planted with a single tropical plant specimen are the proper appendage to a formal garden, large or small. In this garden style, use them in a balanced, geometric arrangement that accentuates the garden's geometry, like four containers at the junction of four corners. Some tropical specimen plants grown in containers enhance non-tropical gardens better than others, such as plumbago, citrus, or orange jessamine (*Murraya paniculata*) sited in a rose garden. These plants appear more like hardy plants than do hot-colored hibiscus or large-leaved palms; their color, texture, and form are harmonious with roses. Nothing is more appropriate for a herb garden than pots of *Aloe vera*, which is grown in gardens throughout the Caribbean for its herbal properties.

When contained plant specimens, especially architectural plants, are elevated on a pedestal and given the prominence they deserve, they become a good focal point to

A cluster of terra-cotta containers with cool-colored plants—*Plectranthus argentatus*, Madagascar periwinkle (*Catharanthus roseus* 'Pink Polka Dot'), *Scaveola ameula* 'Blue Wonder', and *Tradescantia pallida* 'Purple Heart'—cascading over the rim, are arranged informally on this brick patio.

terminate an axis or a vertical accent in the center of a tropical lawn bed. For informal settings, an informal arrangement that clusters various container styles with various kinds of plants in them, but of a selected color scheme, is best. Position an arrangement like this near a poolside that isn't geometric (such as a kidney shape) and cluster the containers within the concave side of the pool.

Tender plants in containers are versatile; move them outdoors for the summer months and indoors for the wintertime, as they do at the palace of Versailles and have done since the days of the Sun King. Every spring wooden tubs of citrus, date palms, and pomegranates are marched outdoors and positioned into grand formal boulevards. When weather starts to chill in the autumn, the plants retreat to the protection of the orangerie, a structure with glass on its south-facing facade, until the following spring.

Container culture like this has been practiced for centuries, so why not continue the legacy? Your garage can double for an orangerie, albeit less elegantly than Versailles. Convert a corner that isn't bothered by frost into a winter home for subtropical plants that benefit from, or don't mind, a winter chill, such as the lily-of-the-nile (*Agapanthus africanus*), New Zealand flax, oleander, pomegranate, and, of course, citrus. These plants will even withstand a touch of frost.

All about Containers

When planting a container garden, you need to consider both the plants and the vessel they grow in. If the total effect is to look good, the plants and the container must both look good and be right for each other. For this to occur, you need to consider carefully the size, style, and material of the container and select the best one for your garden from the multitude that exist.

How Much Room Should a Root Ball Have?

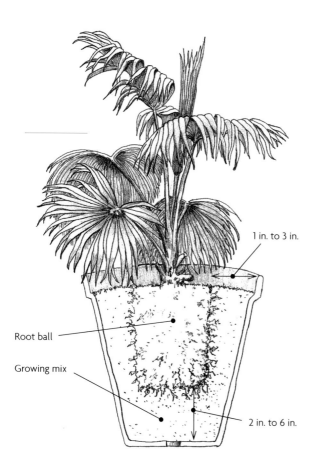

1 in. to 3 in.

Root ball

Growing mix

2 in. to 6 in.

Container size

When selecting (or building) a container, regardless of style or material, the principal consideration must be size. If the container is too small, the plant inside it will suffer and may not survive the entire growing season, no matter how well you maintain it. When plants are crowded into a small pot, or an old specimen has outgrown its pot, the roots become tightly matted together and quickly use all available water. The plant's root system needs as much room to grow as available space and aesthetic proportion will allow. So choose a pot size at least 2 in., and with some vigorous plants as much as 6 in., wider and deeper than the root ball (see the drawing at left). Shallow containers benefit only fibrous-rooted plants, those without thick tuberous roots, that prefer dry conditions. In general, when choosing containers for tropical plants outdoors, bigger is better.

Determine what size fits best into the garden. The container must be in scale with the space, not too big and not too small, and the plant must be in scale with the container. Whatever size container is selected, be certain there are drainage holes in its base. The more holes there are, the happier the plants will be, so drill additional holes into the bottom of wooden and concrete containers. A 3-ft.-diameter container can easily accommodate fifteen ½-in. holes.

Container style

After you've determined the right size for your container, you can then choose its style, which might be as natural as a hollowed-out tree stump, as artful as museum sculpture, or as simple as a large flowerpot. Although the container style is mostly a matter of personal taste, try to match the container to the style of the garden space or adjacent architecture.

Right: Informal, rustic containers are simply made from twigs or branches that retain their bark.

Below: This rolled-rim terra-cotta container is promiscuously planted with chartreuse and variegated plants.

For example, if your garden is symmetric and formal and your home is in the Georgian or Federal style, a pair of classical-styled containers constructed in a material that imitates marble or bronze is more appropriate than a rustic receptacle carved out of a tree stump or made from unbarked twigs like willow or grape vines. Rustic planters are informal and are best clustered with other wooden containers, like bourbon barrels, near a simple, unpretentious dwelling.

Container styles that imitate the designs of ancient Greece and Rome are artful and become garden sculpture. The proportion of their form is as pleasing to the eye as the proportion of a golden-mean rectangle. In the 17th century, the classical urn form became a popular ornament in the gardens of the European aristocracy, and since then countless copies have been made. In America, the urn or "vase" form has embellished gardens since the middle of the 19th century and continues to do so. Sometimes, exuberant scrolling handles were added to reflect the rococo taste or rectilinear ones to associate with the reforms of the Arts and Crafts period. Serpents, swans, cranes, and dragon-shaped attachments suggest the exoticism of the Orient, both delicate and aesthetic, and are a great accompaniment to exotic tropicals.

Container material

Each size and style of container is manufactured in a seemingly infinite number of materials. For example, the classic Grecian-style container can be found in marble, bronze, cast iron, poured concrete, terra-cotta, plastic, and fiberglass. Each material has its own merit. You must consider which manufactured material will best complement the aesthetic of the style, provide the best environment for plant growth, and still be affordable. Sound easy? It's not. Selecting a container is the most daunting task of container gardening.

Containers made from baked earth, or "terra-cotta," have been a part of gardens since ancient times. They offer plants a good growing environment. Clay pots are porous; air passes through the pot into the mix and benefits root growth. However, water vapor also passes through, and out of, the pot. Soil mixes dry faster than in nonporous containers, so it is necessary to water plants frequently in clay pots. The porous surface of clay also holds moisture that may freeze during the winter and

Terra-cotta pots and whiskey barrels are good receptacles for palm trees that are picturesquely positioned on a lawn at Wave Hill, Bronx, New York. From left to right: Chinese fan palm (*Livistona chinensis*), pygmy date palm (*Phoenix roebelinii*), and the Mediterranean fan palm (*Chamaerops humilis*).

crack the container. To protect clay pots from winter breakage, bring them indoors or turn empty containers upside-down and cover with a tarp. They are affordable but fragile and require winter protection.

Wooden bourbon or whiskey barrels, cut in half, are almost as traditional a receptacle for exotic plants as terra-cotta. Old garden books often illustrate plants like *Agapanthus* and palms within them. I don't find bourbon barrel tubs as handsome as warm-colored terra-cotta pots, but large plant specimens don't mind the difference. And wooden barrels don't break. Use them in a rustic or informal setting.

At Versailles, elegant square-sided wooden tubs constructed of vertically aligned boards painted white or green are used to grow specimen citrus trees, date palms, and pomegranates. One side is hinged and acts as a door. When plants are in need of repotting, it is only necessary to open the door, root prune, remove old soil, and add fresh soil mix around the root ball. The plant doesn't have to be moved.

Lightweight plastic containers are nonporous, so the soil doesn't dry as quickly as in terra-cotta containers. They are inexpensive but can look cheap. Some plastic containers effectively imitate clay, bringing less weight and winter durability to the terra-cotta standard.

Fiberglass is a promising container material. It is lightweight, overwinters without protection, is moderately priced, and insulates plant roots from temperature extremes. Many fiberglass pots are cast to look like marble, bronze, and clay. Concrete can be poured into different molds to produce different styles of durable, heavy containers. They overwinter outdoors without protection. Some are colored to resemble terra-cotta.

Cast-iron containers can be as artful as marble or bronze, especially when tropicals like *Yucca elephantipes* 'Variegata', *Chlorophytum comosum* 'Vittatum', and *Salvia splendens* are grown in them, in a proper growing mix, with proper maintenance. This container is in the Smithsonian Garden, Washington, D.C.

Marble or bronze containers are artful and elegant but usually too costly to consider. In the 1850s, like today, the American middle class could not afford marble or bronze, so the new cast-iron industry manufactured affordable vases from molten ore that rivaled the sculptor's chisel. The vases were then painted to imitate marble or bronze. Cast-iron containers like these are still manufactured in styles that were popular a century ago, but the prices are less affordable than they once were. Cast-iron containers are beautiful, but they are heavy, cumbersome, and breakable.

Container Culture

As a rule, plants prefer to grow in the open earth rather than within a confined container. The limited growing space of a container, combined with fluctuating soil temperatures and variable levels of water, oxygen, and nutrients, creates an environment for plants that is stressful. Contained plants must rely totally on gardeners for all their water and nutrient needs, since there isn't a large patch of soil with abundant reserves nearby. The container, its growing mix, and the maintenance practices provided must all be designed to combat the unnatural conditions of the container environment.

Growing mixes

Containerized plants grow best in an artificial growing mix that retains water, nutrients, and oxygen for root growth. It is a mixture of soil and/or soil-like ingredients. If garden soils and packaged topsoils are used alone in a container, they drain poorly and hold too much water, which pushes oxygen out of the soil.

Since the critical factor in container culture is moisture—too little or too much—it is essential that the growing mix contain large pore spaces that will hold water, nutrients, and oxygen yet permit fast drainage (see the drawing at right). Large pore spaces also keep the mix from tightly packing around the plant roots.

Growing mixes are typically made up of three components. The first is organic matter, such as sphagnum peat moss or compost, which helps the mix to retain water and nutrients. The second component is coarse particles such as perlite, vermiculite, calcined clay (Turface), fine bark chips, or sand. They form the large pore spaces and drainage capillaries throughout the depth of the growing mix that facilitate the flow of water and air. The third, and sometimes optional, component of growing mixes is sterilized topsoil. Generally I add sterilized topsoil to lightweight mixes that consist of only peat moss and perlite to create a mix that is one-third of each component. The topsoil prolongs the life of the media, adds nutrients and water-holding capacity, and provides additional weight and root support. (Plants are less apt to topple in the wind.)

Container gardeners don't have to prepare their own growing mix. Scientifically blended premixed formulas that provide the best root environment for inside a container are avail-

Pore Spaces

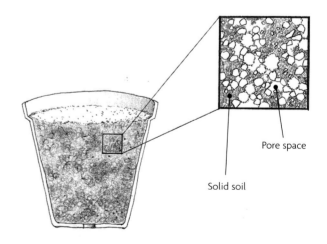

Solid soil

Pore space

When coarse particles in the growing mix abut each other, pore spaces form between them. These pore spaces connect together to form drainage capillaries through which water and oxygen pass.

Growing-Mix Formulas

The formula for the growing mix you need depends on the length of time the plants are to remain in the container. For example, a seasonal display of temporary plants, like the wishbone flower (*Torenia fournieri*), spends fewer months in the growing mix than permanent plants, like the Chinese fan palm (*Livistona chinensis*) that you plan to overwinter indoors without repotting. If the plants are to remain in the container environment less than nine months, the mix can have a high (50%) sphagnum peat moss content. However, after about nine months of supporting plant growth, sphagnum peat moss begins to decompose and pore spaces begin to compact, which means that too much water is retained and oxygen is expelled.

Plants that will remain in containers longer than nine months need growing-mix formulations with less sphagnum peat moss and more coarse particles, like fine bark chips or calcined clay (a soil amendment that looks like kitty litter). These formulations decompose more slowly and keep pore spaces open longer. If you have a prepared growing mix with a high percentage of sphagnum peat moss, add about 20% fine bark chips or calcined clay for these plants.

able at garden centers. Usually the formula lasts only one season outdoors, and then the mix begins to deteriorate.

There's a long-standing tradition that you should place a layer of coarse material, like crushed stone, gravel, or broken crockery, at the bottom of a container to speed drainage. However, when a growing mix with ample pore spaces is used, a drainage layer is not necessary and may even be harmful. A film of water can form between the drainage layer and the mix, causing the pore spaces near it to fill with water and hamper drainage. This is more critical in shallow containers (those less than 16 in. deep). If a coarse material layer is used at the bottom of a deep container, separate it from the mix with a landscape mulching mat or screen to permit free passage of water without soil loss.

Remember, if holes aren't in the bottom of the container to allow water to exit, the very best growing mix will fail. The more holes that are in a container, the faster the water will exit. If

In a New York garden each spring, new plants of *Mandevilla* x *amoena* 'Alice du Pont' are purchased and planted in terra-cotta containers, in fresh growing mix, and fertilized weekly with a liquid formulation. Vines then twine 8 ft. to 10 ft. through the rustic gazebo.

Containers often need a complete watering every day.

Dense foliage can funnel water away from the container, and the small amount of growing mix in the container can't hold as much water as your garden soil can.

The best and easiest way to check if your container needs water is to poke a finger into the growing mix. If it's dry, water. If it's damp, check again tomorrow. It would be convenient if plants could be watered on a predictable schedule, but unfortunately there are several factors that determine how quickly plants use water. In June, when days are long and tropicals are in active growth, they may need three times as much water as they will in September. Containers sitting in constant sun and wind dry quickly and need more water than containers in damp shade, as do containers that are packed full of plants or with old, root-bound specimens inside them. Certain plants, like those in the aroid family (caladium) will also require more water than drought-tolerant euphorbias.

To thoroughly water any container that has drainage holes, wait to water until the growing mix becomes slightly dry. Then water at the center of the container until water comes through the drainage holes. Be certain the water soaks into the mix first and doesn't just run out the sides of the container. Don't be afraid to give plants a good soaking twice a day, especially in hot, dry weather.

Leaves love water too, and one way they can get it is through misting. Turn your hose onto a fine spray and coat the leaves. Misting cleans the leaves and increases the humidity around the plants, which is beneficial for many tropical plants. Mist plants in the morning when they are not in direct sunlight, so they don't burn in the hot afternoon sun.

the 6-in. plastic flowerpots used by greenhouse growers contain eight holes, a 3-ft.-diameter outdoor container can easily accommodate fifteen to twenty ½-in. holes.

Watering

When things get dry inside a container, roots don't have access to the water reserves held deep in garden soils. They depend on you to supply the additional water needed to remain healthy and lush. Even when the rainfall seems sufficient to satisfy your borders and beds, check to see if your container mixes are wet.

To conserve moisture levels in containers, consider using mulches. Mulching is especially useful in containers with multiple plants or plants that are drought intolerant. A 2-in. to 3-in. soil surface cover will not only reduce evaporation but also stabilize soil temperature and reduce weed seed germination. Choose a mulch for containers carefully; particle size should be small—no larger than 1 in. in diameter. Coarse wood chips aren't a good choice, but cocoa hulls, pea gravel, shredded bark, shredded oak leaves, or shredded corn cobs are. Don't use peat moss, which repels water when it dries, or sawdust, which robs nitrogen from the soil as it decomposes.

Fertilizing

Tropical plants, like all plants, require nutrients for their growth. In the jungle, nutrients are recycled into the soil from the rapid decomposition of leaves that fall from the trees to the soil surface below. But few of the leaves that fall from the tropical plants growing in your containers actually reach the soil surface, and fewer still decompose quickly enough to return nutrients into the growing mix. You need to fertilize tropical plants in container environments to provide them with the nutrients they require for growth.

Most fertilizers, either dry or liquid, supply the three nutrients (nitrogen, phosphorus, and potassium) that are required by the plant in the greatest quantity. They are represented in varying ratios by three numbers on the fertilizer package in the order of nitrogen (N), phosphorus (P), and potassium (K). For example, a fertilizer with the ratio 5-10-5, contains 5% nitrogen, 10% phosphorus as phosphoric acid, and 5% potassium as potash. The dry fertilizer, superphosphate 0-18-0, supplies only phosphorus, no nitrogen or potassium.

Nitrogen is the nutrient plants use to produce leafy growth, so large tropical foliage plants benefit from nitrogen fertilizers. The nitrogen component of many fertilizers is from either calcium nitrate, potassium nitrate, or urea. However, nitrogen from these sources quickly leaches from the soil and, if applied above the recommended dose, will burn and kill plant roots. To supply containers with nitrogen for the entire growing season you need to use a slow-release fertilizer.

Slow-release fertilizers are either organic or synthetically produced. In the organic types, natural materials of plant and animal origin, such as compost, bonemeal, or dried manure, decompose slowly and gradually release their nutrients into the growing mix over several months. Synthetically produced slow-release fertilizers have sustained release patterns that range from three months to several years.

Mix spheres of plastic-encapsulated fertilizer into the growing mix before planting or cultivate into the surface afterward (as shown).

Container plants can be combined to look like a tropical border. Clockwise from left to right: coleus, variegated abutilon, *Euphorbia cotinifolia,* angel wing begonia, bromeliad, and variegated impatiens.

When incorporated into the growing mix prior to planting, slow-release fertilizers provide all the necessary nitrogen, phosphorus, and potassium for that season.

"Osmocote" is a common example of a plastic-encapsulated slow-release fertilizer. It consists of plastic spheres that resemble caviar but are filled with a dry, water-soluble fertilizer (see the photo on p. 99). Once water penetrates the capsule, its walls form fissures, and the fertilizer slowly passes out into the growing mix. The longevity of "Osmocote" is controlled by the composition of the fertilizer and the thickness of the capsule wall. Different formulations release nutrients for different lengths of time.

For my tropical containers I use a balanced "Osmocote" blend like 14-14-14 or 10-10-10 (nitrogen-phosphorus-potassium) that will release nutrients into the media for a three-month to four-month period. Although slow-release fertilizers like "Osmocote" and organic materials like dried manure provide complete nutrition, to boost plant growth I supplement them with a dilute (50%) weekly application of a dissolved liquid fertilizer, like Peter's 10-10-10 or "Miracle-Gro," beginning about two weeks after planting. I do this when I water during the months of June and July, when days are long, temperatures are warm, and plants are in active growth. Since liquid fertilizers quickly leach from the soil, they require continued applications to remain effective.

Container Plants

Containers function as focal points that are quick to capture your attention, not blend into the background. So container plants must be focal plants with big bright blossoms, large leaves, and stiff stems; hot colors, coarse

Container Topiary

Since containers are man-made environments, it is especially appropriate to plant man-made forms, such as topiary, in them. Fruit trees, like pomegranates and citrus, pruned into a single stem with a globose head (what we call a "standard") remind me of gardens near the Mediterranean Sea. Similar effects can be achieved with a related plant that grows in Caribbean gardens, the orange jessamine. It responds well to pruning, which stimulates the plant to produce its sweet-scented flowers. Those gardeners who are not timid with secaturs soon discover that lots of species can be trained into standards.

Dwarf pomegranates (*Punica granatum* 'Nana') can be sheared into a globular sphere, whereas single-stemmed standards can be developed from taller varieties. Leave them outdoors in the autumn until the plants defoliate, and then move the containers into a cold garage for winter.

Trained standards of the calamondin orange (x*Citrofortunella microcarpa*) are commercially available at nurseries and garden centers. During the winter they are good houseplants in front of a cool, sunny window. In spring, shear the foliage head to keep it round.

textures, and architectural forms. Container plants can be used singly as a specimen or mixed into an exotic array, as in a large floral arrangement or a tropical border. Here, the design elements—color, texture, and form—will dictate the plant choice and their arrangement in the composition.

Architectural specimen plants

The most architectural of all containers, those in the classic Grecian style, look best when they are planted with the most architectural of all plants, like *Agave americana* or *Yucca elephantipes*. These plants are as sculptural as the vase, and together they become part of the garden architecture. Plant just a single specimen in the center of the vase, and then use it as a focal point to terminate an axis.

Agave americana, also called American aloe, is a bold and brassy succulent. From the heart of this rigid specimen emerge thick and leathery leaves, 3 ft. to 6 ft. long, that twist and snake then cascade down the side of the container. The familiar color is silvery blue-green, but leaves of the cultivar *Agave americana* 'Marginata' sport a yellow margin and those of *Agave americana* 'Medio-picta', a yellow center.

Agave and *Yucca* require little water and are easy to maintain, so they are good plant choices for Grecian-style vases that have a narrow diameter and a relatively small planting space that may dry quickly (see the illustration on the facing page). These exotic Mexican desert dwellers survive drought conditions in barren soil. They tolerate lots of neglect but will reward good cultivation—a proper growing mix, water, and fertilizer—with speedy growth.

The common name, century plant, refers to *Agave*'s reputed flowering habit—only once a century. However, when given favorable growing conditions, amazing flower stalks, up to 20 ft. tall, can emerge in fewer than 10 years. Should your *Agave* flower, be pleasantly surprised—but don't expect it. After the event, the plant will die, but a profusion of "pups" forms at its base to ensure continuity.

While the leaves of *Yucca elephantipes* are still stiff as a spear, it is one of the spineless members of its genus and less sinister than *Agave americana*.

Fig. 4.—Agave Americana.

Throughout the 19th century, *Agave americana* was the recommended plant for Grecian-style containers.

Pineapples, either *Ananas comosus* 'Variegatus' or *Ananas bracteatus* 'Tricolor', are as effective a single specimen as *Agave* for the center stage of any style container, but they are perfect in a Grecian-styled one. These relatives of bromeliads are architectural plants that possess a strong symmetrical outline. Serrated leaves about 3 ft. long whorl from the heart of the plant and cascade over the container's edge. As tempted as you may be, don't grow the heads of grocery-store pineapples. The ornamental cultivars, not grown for their fruit but for delicious cream and pink stripes that ribbon down the length of the leaf like candy, are far more beautiful.

Pandanus is as sculptural as *Agave* or pineapple. It is a strange genus of ornamental trees and

Nancy Goodwin grows an architectural pineapple *(Ananas comosus* 'Variegatus') in a Grecian-style cast-iron vase at Montrose Gardens, North Carolina.

Spines that can rip your skin like a knife line the edge of all *Agave americana* leaves, and a dangerous stiff needle is at the leaf apex. In public spaces or where children run, be careful where these plants are placed. The vase needs to top a plinth so the agave leaf is above eye level.

large shrubs native to East Indian islands and Madagascar. Linear leaves are long, 3 ft. to 5 ft., and spearlike. They're similar to pineapple leaves. On some species, the leaf edge is spiny and the leaf is truly like a spear. But don't be dissuaded from growing it. The leaf arrangement, overlapping at the base then spiraling around the stem, forms a plant of extraordinary architecture that is appropriate for the center of a container. After the leaves fall, the scars resemble the threads of a screw, and contribute toward its common name, "screw pine." In some species leaves are striped, either white (*Pandanus veitchii*) or gold (*Pandanus baptistii* 'Aurea').

Just as remarkable as the foliage are the thick, aerial prop roots that project from the side of the stem at an angle, grow downward, and enter the soil to support the plant. *Pandanus* plants grow in full sun and in moist conditions, but they acclimate to shade and tolerate some drought.

Mixed planting arrangements

The arrangement of plants in containers with wide diameters can simulate the arrangement of plants in a tropical lawn bed: the tallest kinds in the center, then shorter and fuller varieties that slope outward and downward like a pyramid, and, finally, those that will cascade over the edge. The finest display occurs when a container designed in this manner is placed on a pedestal, in the center of the tropical lawn bed that it is simulating.

In the center of a wide-diameter container, plant upright forms such as *Cordyline indivisa* or *Cordyline fruticosa* (which were common 19th-century center spikes) or plants trained into symmetric forms, such as topiary. Around them fill the space with bedding plants of spherical forms like *Alternanthera ficoidea, Iresine herbstii,* or coleus. Then, prostrate plants, such as the wandering jew, can cascade over the vase's rim.

Grown outdoors, the wandering jew (*Tradescantia zebrina*) is dense and vibrant, not spindly and dusty as it inevitably becomes when grown indoors. It loses its commonness and is a splendid garden plant. The succulent stems mat together to hide the soil, then drape down the sides of their container. Flat leaves, about 2 in. long and 1 in. wide, are striped with two silver bands. Upper leaf surfaces shimmer like steel, the under surfaces like a concord grape. These plants are determined to grow. Failure with them is near impossible. They flourish in the damp shade, but should they wander into

PAINTED FOR VICKS MONTHLY
CARDEN VASE.

An architectural plant, like cordyline or dracaena, is in the center of this wide-diameter vase. Elephant's ears and coleus surround it, and annual nasturtiums cascade over the rim. (From *Vick's Monthly Magazine,* 1880.)

full sunshine, they are even better. Sunlight stimulates purple pigment production and intensifies the leaf color.

If you prefer arrangements that display less geometry, plant your container promiscuously.

Dracaena reflexa 'Song of India' highlights the center of a contemporary container in dappled shade at Wave Hill, Bronx, New York. Coleus surrounds it, and *Helichrysum petiolare* 'Limelight' cascades over the container's rim.

Design a harmonious mass that displays a variety of foliage and flowers. Plan the blooms to mingle and cluster thickly in well-contrasted or blended colors, as shown in the photo above.

Vines

For most gardeners, vines convey images of picturesque cottages clad with fragrant flowers. Sometimes these visions are apt, but not in the tropics. Despite their romance and grace, vines in tropical environments are invasive and often downright weedy. They need control. They need to be contained. So it seems appropriate to grow them within the confines of a terra-cotta pot, which will often trigger these plants into flower. Vines like *Bougainvillea* and *Tecomaria capensis* remain vegetative when grown in moist, rich soil. It takes the stress from alternating wet and dry conditions that frequently occurs in terra-cotta containers to change their growth pattern from producing foliage to flowers.

Vines overcome their unruly nature when you give them a frame on which to grow; you force them into an architectural form. Then their height strengthens the garden's third dimension. To create a vine support, try putting a vine tepee into the pot. Take three bamboo stakes at least 6 ft. long and tie them together at their top with twine (see the photo at right on the facing page). Now you can train the vine into a topiary form, like a cone, pyramid, or cylinder.

Vines have different methods of climbing their way to the sun. The most common way is to twine; round and round they go, then up, up, and away. Stems of twining vines coil and wrap around other plants like a snake. *Thunbergia alata* vigorously twines and covers other plants like prey as it reaches for brighter sunlight, but twiners like *Mandevilla* x *amoena* 'Alice du Pont' are much less invasive. Others, such as *Passiflora*, are held at higher elevations by a modified leaf or tendril that twists around objects and other plants. They are among the best vines to train in containers.

Clinging vines, like golden pothos, produce roots along their stem that adhere it to another surface. Some vines, such as *Allamanda cathartica* or *Solandra maxima*, simply produce long, weak stems like jungle cables. Bougainvillea's long stems have thorns to hook them onto some kind of support.

To achieve a full specimen look from slower growing vines, like *Stephanotis floribunda*, plants need to mature over several years through overwintering. Vines like *Mandevilla* x *amoena* 'Alice du Pont' and *Urechites lutea* will provide an adequate show in a single growing season but become splendid plants in their second and third years. And some vines like *Thunbergia alata* are too vigorous to consider growing for a second year.

Vines like this variegated bougainvillea flower better when they become pot-bound in a clay container. If planted in rich, fertile soil, leaves grow at the expense of flowers.

Before potting twining vines like *Mandevilla* x *amoena* 'Alice du Pont' (above) or the yellow mandevilla, *Urechites lutea,* fashion together a tripod from bamboo stakes for them to grow on.

Although no rule prohibits growing other plants with vines, I generally plant vines singly in a container, or perhaps two or three different kinds with similar vigor. Vining plants tend to attack and conquer nonviners, so I try to prevent future battles and provide clear direction. When vines are grown as specimen plants in a container they are easy to move into a plant room or greenhouse at the end of the growing season; their roots aren't anchored into ground soil and their stems haven't twisted onto nonmobile supports. Just prune away excess stem growth that grows out of control.

As the years pass, keep your container garden stimulating by sampling new plants. A diverse group of tropicals appropriate for containers is available in nurseries each spring. Like my first tropical container, they can be simple massed plantings of vibrant annual plants, like the wishbone flower *Torenia,* or they can be more complex compositions. Since most annual plants originate in the tropics, they are at home with exotic-looking tropicals. Pots brimming with petunias can be as picturesque as fronds of palm waving in the wind. Use them together on your patio or poolside to form images of islands in the sea.

6 Growing Tropical Plants

Good gardens don't just happen, they are made. Whether you are planting hardy flowering plants, fruits and vegetables, or exotic tropicals, the process is essentially the same throughout the growing season. The soil needs to be prepared, plants need watering and pruning, and, unfortunately, weeds still need to be pulled. The greatest difference in caring for a tropical garden comes at the beginning and end of the season, when tropicals need to be protected from cooler temperatures.

Planting

Before you can plant your border or bed, you need to prepare its soil thoroughly. Soil preparation is critical for the success of any garden, but especially for a garden of tropical plants where fast growth is encouraged. Since the life span of the tropical garden is limited, you want to speed the development of its plants to get the longest enjoyment from them. Digging the soil to a depth of about 16 in. and then adding organic matter and fertilizer stimulates roots to grow deeper into the soil. Moisture-retentive organic matter reduces the chance of drought stress, and its rich, dark color warms the soil fast in spring since it absorbs the sun's rays.

The best time to prepare the soil is late summer or early autumn, to allow time for it to settle before next year's planting. You can prepare soil and plant tropicals in the same season, but sometimes spring soils are too wet to allow adequate preparation. For complete soil preparation procedures, follow the directions given in chapter 3.

When to plant

Be guided by local night temperatures to determine when to plant the tropical garden. Most plants can go outdoors when night temperatures remain above 60°F, or preferably 65°F. This is usually between May 15 and June 5 in zone 6, when tomatoes (which are tropical plants) are also planted. Species native to higher elevations, like *Abutilon pictum* 'Thompsonii', *Brugmansia* x *candida,* and *Tecomaria capensis,* don't mind cooler temperatures and can go outdoors when night temperatures remain above 50°F. Consult the glossary for other plants that may give your garden a head start.

After tapping *Colocasia esculenta* 'Fontanesii' out of its pot (top), gently separate the roots and remove excess potting mix (middle). Position plants into a hole larger than the root mass that has been loosened with a fork or spade (bottom).

Just because you're eager to get into the spring sunshine doesn't mean that your tropical plants are also ready. Many need to be acclimated to outdoor sunlight before they enter a sunny garden; otherwise, their foliage will sunburn and drop. Plants grown in full-sun greenhouse conditions are already acclimated and can be planted directly into a sunny garden. But if your plants spent the winter in a dim garage, basement, or even on a north-facing windowsill, or if they've been grown in nurseries for houseplant culture, they need to be introduced to full sunlight slowly. Prune away dead and weak growth, and then, when night temperatures are warm enough, bring plants outdoors and place them in the shade. They can receive the faintest rays of sunlight in the earliest and latest hours of the day. Over the next two weeks, gradually move the pots into positions where they will receive increased amounts of sunlight.

An alternative acclimation method that eliminates moving plants like musical chairs (which becomes difficult with large and heavy containers) is to position plants where they belong and then cover them with a loose-textured burlap, cheesecloth, or horticultural screening cloth (it's a bit like using a protective sunscreen). Tie the screen on for one to two weeks and then uncover the plants on a cloudy day. To avoid damage from strong spring sunshine, it's always best to bring plants outdoors on a cloudy or, better yet, misty day.

How to plant

Before you plant them permanently, position plants on top of the prepared soil to be sure you like their arrangement. Start with large specimens and architectural plants, as shown in the bottom photo at right. When you're certain the plants are in their correct spot, go

To acclimate pots of the Chinese fan palm (*Livistona chinensis*) to the bright June sun, the author covers them with an old sheer curtain before they leave the greenhouse.

Large specimens, like the bananas, are planted first.

Roots of this pot-bound butterfly ginger (*Hedychium coronarium*) are teased apart with a hand cultivator to encourage new roots to grow out of the potting mix and into the garden soil.

ahead and plant them. Then position and plant medium-sized plants followed by the smallest plants. You're less apt to damage small plants if they enter the soil last.

Most times I remove the plant from its pot, especially if repotting is needed or if I want the plant to increase in size dramatically during the growing season. Tropicals grow more vigorously in prepared garden soil than in containers (where stressful conditions occur more frequently). Plants that are in ill health and need rejuvenation go directly into the outdoor soil.

I transplant pot-bound specimens into larger containers or directly into the garden soil. You'll know a plant is pot-bound when the root mass mimics the form of the flowerpot. To prepare it for garden planting, lightly tease the roots apart with the least amount of root breakage, as shown in the photo above.

Bringing a plant outdoors into sun, wind, and rain is enough of a shock for it to have to recover from, so avoid excess root manipulation at this time. I gently rub the root mass with my hand, breaking fibrous roots free from the soil mass. This encourages new roots to grow outward into the freshly prepared soil.

When you're ready to plant, dig a hole larger than the root mass, making sure the soil in the bottom of the hole is loose and friable. For plants whose growth I want to accelerate, I mix a slow-release fertilizer (such as "Osmocote") into the bottom of the hole and into the backfill. This is in addition to the dry superphosphate and 5-10-5 (nitrogen-phosphorus-potassium) fertilizer I used in soil preparation (see p. 52).

To achieve the correct planting depth, position the plant's crown at the same soil level in the ground as it was in its pot. The roots of some

From Pot to Soil

Dig the planting hole wider and deeper than the root mass.

Loosen the bottom soil and return amended soil into it.

Position the teased root mass into the hole's center, making certain the plant is straight. Return and grade the soil.

the remainder into the backfill. When wet, this compound absorbs water and becomes jelly-like. Plant roots grow into the jelly and remain moist longer.

Plants that are difficult to transplant, like palms, or those that you don't want to increase in size can be planted outdoors into the soil without removing their pot. Sometimes the pot simply sits on the soil surface, which creates the illusion of a taller plant.

pot-bound plants push the crown above the pot's soil level, a condition common with palms. In these instances, plant the roots deeper so that the plant's crown is level with the garden soil. Plants that root easily from their stem, like coleus, can be planted slightly deeper than they were in their pot.

You can fine-tune each planting hole to create ideal growing conditions for individual species. For example, I amend the soil for plants that like it wet, like *Colocasia esculenta* and *Cyperus alternifolius*, with a water-absorbent planting gel. For holes about 12 in. wide and 12 in. deep, I use about 3 oz. to 4 oz. of the dry material, mixing half throughout the planting hole and

At SUNY Farmingdale, the variegated pineapple, *Ananas comosus* 'Variegatus', (far right) is placed on top of the soil surface in its pot to create the illusion of a taller plant.

Water tropicals (here, *Colocasia esculenta* 'Fontanesii') immediately after planting and then as needed, which may be several times a week.

Maintenance

As with any garden, the watchword for tending a tropical garden is diligence. Since tropical plants pour all their energy into one powerful but short season, they grow tremendously, which means gardeners have to be ready with water, fertilizer, and pruning shears. But the reward of season-long blooms and luxuriant foliage is well worth the effort.

Watering and fertilizing

Tropicals should be watered immediately after planting and then as needed. As plants age and grow, larger root masses and leaf surfaces absorb and use more water than young plants do. When weather conditions are sunny and windy, soil water evaporates faster and you'll need to apply water more frequently.

I'm old-fashioned and still water with hoses and sprinklers, partly because I like to see plants washed with water from above like a tropical shower and partly because hoses are easier to manipulate than a complex irrigation system. Overhead sprinkling also increases the humidity level, which suits tropical plants. It takes at least four to six hours of sprinkling to penetrate the dense midsummer foliage canopy and wet the soil deeply. Plants require *at least* 1 in. of water per week. If you are uncertain about how much water actually falls to the ground, place coffee cans throughout the garden and measure the depth of accumulated water. I often let water trickle from the hose at the base of thirsty plants, like *Colocasia esculenta*, whose large leaves consume and transpire lots of water. Soaker hoses are good for this kind of irrigation.

Two weeks after planting, boost plants with a readily available liquid fertilizer, such as Peter's 10-10-10 (nitrogen-phosphorus-potassium) or "Miracle-Gro," at a more dilute rate (about 50%) than the recommendation. Greenhouse or garden-center plants were receiving continuous liquid fertilization before you bought them, and now they're ready for more. I'm impatient and want a lush garden fast, so I liquid-feed every week or two until August. On plants I'm especially eager to "push," like bananas and *Colocasia esculenta*, I'll also sprinkle a granular 10-6-4 around their base.

Pests: No More than the Standard Fare

The tropical garden looks like Eden, but it has its share of problems, just as any garden does. The good news is that pests and diseases don't occur any more frequently in tropical gardens than in annual, perennial, or vegetable gardens. In fact, you have a greater chance of plant injury to cold night temperatures that hover in the 40s and low 50s than to the onslaught of bugs or fungus.

The key to controlling pests and diseases in a tropical garden is to be on the lookout for the same culprits you already have in your garden. If Japanese beetles chew your roses, they'll probably find something to nibble in the tropical garden, like hibiscus blossoms or canna leaves. If soilborne fungus diseases like the water molds *Phythium* and *Phytophthora* were present in your garden before planting tropicals, you may still have to contend with them. (Check the plant glossary entries for specific pests or diseases that some plants are prone to.) The same remedies that work for other plants may also work for tropicals, so consult a good pest and disease reference and read the manufacturer's instructions on any chemical you may use.

Here are some ways to prevent pest and disease in any garden:

• Purchase only pest- and disease-free plants from nurseries.

• Water early in the morning and allow adequate air circulation in the garden for plants to dry before nightfall.

• Keep plants well watered and weed-free. Stressed plants are more susceptible to spider mites and disease.

Weeding and pruning

I like to see a neatly cultivated garden. To me, cultivated soil and cultivated plants are what gardening is all about, and weeding and cultivation are partner practices. After August 1, a properly designed and planted exotic garden should be dense enough that weed growth is inhibited (then you can take a rest), but until that time weed and cultivate.

Fast-growing summer annual weeds are easy to pull and don't bother me as much as perennial weeds like nutsedge. The latter need careful and complete removal of their rhizome and "nut"; otherwise, they'll quickly return. It's important to know what weeds look like and how they grow. Fortunately, most of them don't look tropical and can't be confused with tropical plants.

Until the tropicals grow into each other and cover the soil, weeds need to be removed and the soil needs to be cultivated.

The blue potato bush, *Lycianthes rantonnetii,* (above and at right) is a shrub but can be pruned into a small tree or a topiary. To keep it neat, the crown needs to be pruned back several times during the growing season and shrublike branches need to be removed from the base of the plant.

In the hot and humid tropics, keeping a garden neat is a constant chore. Plants grow quickly and need lots of pruning. During the dog days of a temperate summer, tropical plants react similarly. Continual pruning is necessary, and knowing what and where to pinch or prune is critical. For example, when you pinch the tip of a coleus plant, side shoots grow from axillary buds at the base of the leaves. Tall, leggy plants then become shorter and bushier. Branching from axillary buds occurs more readily on certain plants, like *Alternanthera*. Shearing some shrubby plants like the orange jessamine

(*Murraya paniculata*) results in dense hedge-like growth from its axillary buds. Pruning other shrubs, such as plumbago or the acanth *Barleria cristata,* increases flowering.

Pruning can make some shrubby plants look like a small tree, such as the blue potato bush (*Lycianthes rantonnetii*), shown above, or angel's trumpet *(Brugmansia).* As the plant matures, prune away excess weak stems to train the soft-wooded shrub into a small tree with only a few (one to three) strong, vertical trunks. On

Brugmansia, encourage the leafy canopy to develop into a horizontal umbrella. From the base of each leaf, a 6-in. trumpet-shaped pendulous flower will dangle. Sometimes, a flood of over 200 blossoms hangs like a waterfall. To highlight the flowers, remove excess foliage from the trunk and underplant with a short ground cover like wandering jew.

If you pinch the tip of a herbaceous rhizomatous monocot, like the butterfly ginger *(Hedychium coronarium)* or a heliconia, side branching doesn't occur and the remaining stem will eventually wither back to the rhizome. To shorten a stem on this kind of plant, prune it at ground level, and after flowering. If you're not sure how to prune your tropical plants, consult the glossary.

Just as in the tropics, as new leaves form, old leaves drop to the ground. Almost every summer day in our Tropical Garden at SUNY

Farmingdale there are yellow leaves and spent blossoms to remove, growth to pinch or prune, and fallen leaves to rake up. For me and my gardeners it isn't a constant chore but an exciting experience. The fast growth has created a leafy canopy to crawl beneath and escape to. "This must be what a jungle is like," I imagine as I cut away senescent stems of elephant's ears the size of a pachyderm. Water drips from their leaves above and runs down my back; scents rise from the damp earth. I'm in paradise!

As the weeks of summer come and go and the plants grow and age, remember that you are their boss and must manage the direction of their growth. When one plant is invading its neighbor, don't be afraid to cut it back. Remove annual plants, like *Amaranthus tricolor, Cosmos sulphureus,* or *Tithonia rotundifolia,* when they have completed their life cycle and begin to look seedy. Quick growth is what makes the exotic garden special. And I've fallen victim to its magic.

After the flower finishes, prune the stem of a rhizomatous monocot, like the butterfly ginger, *Hedychium coronarium,* (left) or canna, at ground level. This permits more light to penetrate to the base of the plant and encourages faster growth of new flowering stems.

Overwintering

After Labor Day, it's time to begin making plans for next year's exotic garden. Evaluate what plants were successful this year, what ones you want back next year, and what should be discarded. For the plants you want back next year, determine which ones you'll purchase new in the spring and which ones will be overwintered in a frost-free environment. If certain species are readily available in garden centers, or if they are difficult to overwinter, it's simplest to purchase new plants in May. Attempt to overwinter those tropicals that are not readily available, those you want in larger sizes than are commonly available, and those that survive winter indoors without too much difficulty (in your frost-free garage, for example).

Some plants can overwinter indoors as whole plants, while others that root easily will overwinter as pieces propagated from the original parent plant or perhaps simply as a seed. In zones 7 and 8, where soils don't freeze solid, some plants protected with a mulch will survive the winter outdoors, as a hardy perennial

Overwintering Tropicals: A Sampler

Propagate from cuttings; easy to root and fast growing:
Allamanda schottii
Alternanthera sp.
Cuphea ignea
Hemigraphis alternata
Iresine herbstii
Orthosiphon stamineus
Plectranthus argentatus
Sanchezia speciosa
Tradescantia pallida 'Purple Heart'
Tradescantia zebrina

Overwinter as a houseplant; easy to grow in indoors:
Acalypha hispida
Ananas comosus 'Variegatus'
Codiaeum variegatum pictum
Dracaena marginata 'Tricolor'
Ficus elastica
Livistona chinensis
Musa acuminata 'Dwarf Cavendish'
Pseuderanthemum atropurpureum
Sansevieria fasciata 'Laurentii'
Tradescantia spathacea

Overwinter in a cool garage; larger specimens tolerant of cold:
Brugmansia x *candida*
Cordyline indivisa
Cycas revoluta
Ensete ventricosum
Lantana camara
Nerium oleander
Phormium tenax
Plumbago auriculata
Punica granatum
Tecomaria capensis

Buy new in May; inexpensive and readily available:
Abutilon pictum 'Thompsonii'
Clerodendrum thomsoniae
Crossandra infundibuliformis
Cuphea hyssopifolia
Cyperus alternifolius
Helichrysum petiolare 'Limelight'
Hibiscus acetosella 'Red Shield'
Hypoestes phyllostachya
Mandevilla x *amoena* 'Alice du Pont'
Passiflora coccinea

would. Your best horticultural judgments are needed to put the exotic garden to bed.

Slower-growing plants should be overwintered as whole plants in a frost-free indoor environment. Some can be treated as an interior houseplant and receive artificial light. Others require sunlight either on a windowsill, in a plant room, or in a greenhouse. Some may be content in a cold but frost-free garage or basement with minimum light and water. They're the least bother to overwinter.

Wherever you place them, the plants first need to be dug and potted. Get clean pots and potting mix ready. Then begin to dig the plants. You'll be able to pace yourself, since it's not

Many tropicals, such as *Epipremnum aureum* (shown here), can be dug and potted with fresh growing mix or started new from cuttings and overwintered as a houseplant in front of a window.

Overwintering Setup in a Garage

A frost-free garage, where temperatures hover between 35°F and 50°F, is an ideal environment to overwinter many subtropical and tropical plants that are tolerant of cold.

necessary to dig up the entire garden at once. On an overcast or misty day, when night temperatures begin to hover between 50°F and 55°F (about the middle or end of September in zone 6), start to dig those plants that don't do well in cool night temperatures, like the acanths *Pseuderanthemum* and *Graptophyllum*. Check the glossary for preferred temperatures.

You can pot up plants slowly and continue to enjoy the remaining garden until early October, maybe until Columbus Day. Bring houseplants indoors at least two weeks before you turn on your heat, so they can slowly acclimate to the dry-air interior environment. The plants that will overwinter in the garage, like New Zealand flax, can remain outdoors until November or the first predicted hard frost.

After plants are dug, you'll need to do some pruning. Remove broken leaves, branches, and roots; cut away oversized stems on rhizomatous plants like canna; prune large banana leaves back to the main stem. However, most shrubby plants shouldn't be pruned severely until spring, when longer days return and the renaissance of growth occurs. Terminal buds help to keep the stems alive during low-light winter conditions, so leave them on until spring. When they are removed, branching occurs.

Remove loose soil from the root mass and prune roots that are damaged or too large. I root-prune lantana and abutilon severely, with good results. Using a pot size about 1 in. wider than the diameter of the root mass, pot up the plants with the potting media. Water. Leave

them outdoors in a shady environment to settle. Finally, spray plants that are prone to whiteflies, aphids, or spider mites with an insecticide or miticide before bringing them indoors.

With rhizomatous plants that will overwinter in a bare-root condition (like canna and butterfly ginger), wait until the first frost knocks back their foliage before you remove them from the soil. Then, fork up the 1-in.- to 2-in.-thick and 6-in.- to 12-in.-long rhizomes. Don't divide the clumps until spring. Rinse away soil residues. Once dry, pack the rhizomes in a corrugated cardboard container pierced with air holes, a milk crate, or a wooden vegetable box. Fill dry vermiculite, perlite, peat moss, or excelsior around them. Store them until spring planting in a cool basement or garage at about 45°F to 55°F. Tuberous elephant's ears and caladium are treated similarly.

Propagation

While most tropicals can be overwintered as a large houseplant, those that grow quickly and are easy to propagate, like *Alternanthera* and *Sanchezia,* can be started new from a piece of the original, a stem cutting, in mid to late summer.

To propagate from the parent plant, cut 4-in.-long stem tips at an angle, remove their lower leaves, and uniformly dust their base to a height of 1 in. with a rooting hormone like Hormodin #1, available at garden centers (see the photos on pp. 122-123). Clean and sterilize a plastic container with a 10% bleach solution. Then fill it with a rooting medium such as salt-free sand or perlite. Insert the dusted cuttings into the media in perfect rows, lined up like soldiers. Water. Place the container of

Dig elephant's ears, *Colocasia esculenta,* (far left) after the first frost has killed their leaves (left). Then clean and dry the turnip-like tubers (right).

Propagating a Tropical Plant

Top left: Cut a 4-in.-long stem tip of a plant (such as the Persian shield, *Strobilanthes dyerianus*, shown here) at an angle beneath a leaf node.

Bottom left: Dip the stem base in a rooting hormone powder to a height of about 1 in.

Bottom center: Insert the dusted cutting into a rooting media (such as perlite).

Bottom right: Wait for roots to develop fully (in about eight weeks).

cuttings on a warm and bright, but not sunny, windowsill. Keep the cuttings moist with a clear plastic covering. Monitor for fungal diseases and control any that occur. Pot up plants after roots develop, in about 8 to 12 weeks, and grow on a sunny windowsill until spring. Prune again in March and start more cuttings for May planting.

Windowsill setups are fine to propagate easy-to-root plants, but if propagation becomes your addiction, establish an environment with a heating cable beneath the rooting media; then you'll be able to root a greater number of plant varieties. A warm root zone speeds the rooting process. (Heating cables are available from horticultural supply houses.)

Spring Bulb Gardens

After the tropical plants are brought indoors and the borders or beds are cleaned, raked, and graded for winter, you can give your borders or beds a second life by planting spring bulbs. Borders or beds that are free of the tropical plants make fine places for spring bulb displays, since there are no competing roots to get in the bulbs' way, and vice versa. Historically, tulips, hyacinths, and *Fritillaria imperialis* were grown in Dutch borders and beds; it's how they look best.

Tulips can be planted when soil temperatures dip below 55°F, about the first or second week of November in zone 6. By that time the tropical plants are gone from the tropical garden, the soil has been graded for winter, and you're ready to think of spring. Arrange the bulbs on the empty soil surface, and then trowel them into the soft earth to a depth about three times

A planting of spring bulbs enables tropical borders and tropical beds to serve double-duty.

their length. When they bloom in April and early May, nighttime temperatures are still too cold to consider planting tender tropicals outdoors.

After the bulbs finish flowering, they can be dug and discarded; fresh bulbs are then planted next autumn. Or they can be left in place to bloom a second year. They need about six weeks' dieback time before the foliage can be cut away to ensure the formation of next year's flower bud. Bulb dieback occurs naturally on early-flowering tulips (like the Emperors), *Fritillaria imperialis,* and hyacinths before the tropical plants go outdoors in late May or early June. Late-flowering tulips may be in their way,

Plants that like it hot, such as the variegated cassava (*Manihot esculenta* 'Variegata'), can be protected from cold snaps that occur after they are planted in spring by covering with a pot.

but if you carefully design the bulb display to orchestrate with the tropical planting, there should be no interference.

Spring-flowering bulbs tie together the seasons of the tropical garden from November, when the tropical plants migrate to warmer environments, until their return in May. For the tropi-

cal garden, bulbs are both the encore and the overture, ending one season and starting the next. And, since tulips, hyacinths, and fritillaria are native to distant Near Eastern soils, they're exotic plants too!

A Tropical Plant Glossary

It becomes easier for gardeners to fashion good gardens once they are familiar with the plants they plan to grow. But getting to know plants doesn't happen overnight—and sometimes not even after four seasons of careful tending. This glossary will help you get to know 100 tropical plants—their decorative qualities, sizes, cultural requirements, and uses—so that you can grow tropical plants in a temperate garden more easily. It's not possible to include every tropical plant in the glossary; however, when you become familiar with those that are listed, your exotic garden will be off to a good start.

Using the Glossary

Most people know plants by a common name, but common names vary with the locations where they are given, so that one plant may have several common names. One common name can also refer to several different plants, as with "sage." It is generally associated with the herbal plant used to flavor food, *Salvia officinalis,* but not in the tropics, where "sage" brings to mind the pungent-leaved plant with orange or yellow flowers, *Lantana camara.* To reduce common-name confusion, botanists have developed international standards to name plants scientifically, and those are the names I use in the glossary.

How plants are named

The basis for botanical names is the 1753 publication of the Swedish botanist Linnaeus, *Species Plantarum,* which determines that the botanical name is made from two words, called the binomial. The binomial consists of a generic name, or genus, followed by a specific epithet, or species. The generic name is a noun. It is written in italic, or is underlined, and takes a capital letter. Generic names frequently commemorate someone or are often mythological. They are treated as Latin words, and therefore have gender: masculine, feminine, or neuter. Masculine names most frequently end in "us," like *Asparagus,* feminine names often end in "a," like *Musa,* and neuter names in "um," like *Epipremnum.*

The specific epithet describes individuals with the same or very similar characteristics. When combined with the generic name it becomes the plant's botanical name, its binomial; when used alone it is meaningless. The specific epithet is written in lower case and is italicized or underlined, and, like the generic name, it is treated as a Latin word. It is generally an adjective that sometimes describes the plant, as in the cathartic *Allamanda cathartica,* or its place of origin, like the Chinese fan palm *Livistona chinensis.* Frequently, their word endings agree with those of the generic name, as in *Asparagus densiflorus, Musa acuminata,* or *Epipremnum aureum.*

To comply with international rules of nomenclature, it is sometimes necessary for botanists to change a binomial. For everyone to communicate clearly about the same plant, we need to know both the old, invalid name (the synonym) and the new, valid name. When synonyms exist, I list them in the glossary after the binomial and in parentheses. The binomials used in this book mostly follow those listed in *The New Royal Horticultural Society Dictionary Index of Garden Plants* (Timber Press, 1994) by Mark Griffiths.

When a desirable variant plant arises, or is maintained, in cultivation and keeps its desirable characteristic when reproduced by seed or vegetative means, it is termed a cultivated variety or "cultivar." Cultivar names are printed in Roman script, take a capital first letter, and are enclosed in single quotation marks, as in *Asparagus densiflorus* 'Myersii' or *Musa acuminata* 'Dwarf Cavendish'.

How to find plants

Botanists group together genera that look similar and have similar floral and chemical characteristics into a plant family. And it's how I group plants in the glossary— by their family. This method brings together plants that often have similar identification features (flower form, leaf arrangement, and habit) and many times possess similar cultural requirements. In the glossary, plant families are arranged alphabetically, and within them the genera are alphabetic. Common names are alphabetically indexed to their family at the beginning of the glossary (see pp. 128-129).

Within each entry, features are presented in an outline form that is easy to access. It details the plants' geographic origin, decorative assets of the plants and suggestions on how to use them, how to grow and overwinter them, and what size they may achieve. These features vary. For example, size is a result of the quality of cultural conditions provided and the age of the plant. Young *Abutilon* or *Tibouchina* plants, just rooted the previous spring, do not achieve the tree-like habit in a single growing season that older plants, rooted a year earlier and overwintered, do. Croton plants, commonly available in garden centers in sizes that range from 3 in. to 3 ft., may start their garden life as an edging plant, overwinter on a windowsill, and then move to the rear of the garden the second year.

Sizes listed are approximate for what can be expected in a temperate garden, not the tropics. Rubber plants (*Ficus elastica*) become large trees, 200 ft. tall, in their native southeast Asia or in other nonnative tropical environments, but not in the exotic garden, even if you overwinter them indoors. They may become 8 ft. tall outdoors but then will require pruning if they are to return to the protection of your home. And when you purchase rubber plants, they may be only 18 in. and possibly may double their height in a single growing season. And vines like *Thunbergia grandiflora* are invasive weeds in the tropics covering hundreds of square feet. Never in New York.

Full sun means six to eight hours of unobstructed sunlight. Dappled shade is shade filtered through a tree or shrub. Warm night temperatures are above 60°F, cool nights range between 50°F and 60°F, and cold nights are those below 50°F.

The horticultural uses and combinations proposed are suggestive, and by no means definitive. They are ones I have used, or seen used, with success and are intended to aid your garden design process. But now, as the designer of your own garden, you can create your own plant combinations. Experiment, as I do.

Index of Common Names to Family Names

Common Name	Family Name	Common Name	Family Name
American aloe	Agavaceae	Canna lily	Cannaceae
Angel's trumpet	Solanaceae	Cape honeysuckle	Bignoniaceae
Asparagus fern	Liliaceae	Cape leadwort	Plumbaginaceae
Banana	Musaceae	Caricature plant	Acanthaceae
Beefsteak plant	Amaranthaceae	Castor bean	Euphorbiaceae
Bird of paradise	Strelitziaceae	Castor oil plant	Euphorbiaceae
Black-eyed Susan vine	Acanthaceae	Cat's whiskers	Labiatae
Bleeding heart vine	Verbenaceae	Century plant	Agavaceae
Blood leaf	Amaranthaceae	Chenille plant	Euphorbiaceae
Blue potato bush	Solanaceae	Chicken gizzard	Amaranthaceae
Blue trumpet vine	Acanthaceae	Chinese fan palm	Palmae
Bower of beauty	Bignoniaceae	Cigar flower	Lythraceae
Brazilian jasmine	Apocynaceae	Climbing lily	Liliaceae
Brazilian plume	Acanthaceae	Common allamanda	Apocynaceae
Bridal wreath	Asclepiadaceae	Confederate vine	Polygonaceae
Bush allamanda	Apocynaceae	Copper leaf	Euphorbiaceae
Butterfly bush	Verbenaceae	Coral plant	Scrophulariaceae
Cabbage palm	Agavaceae	Coral vine	Polygonaceae
Caladium	Araceae	Corallita	Polygonaceae
Calamondin orange	Rutaceae	Croton	Euphorbiaceae

Common Name	Family Name	Common Name	Family Name
Dasheen	Araceae	Persian shield	Acanthaceae
Dwarf sago	Cycadaceae	Philippine violet	Acanthaceae
Eddoe	Araceae	Pigeon berry	Verbenaceae
Egyptian star cluster	Rubiaceae	Polka-dot plant	Acanthaceae
Elephant's ears	Araceae	Pomegranate	Punicaceae
Elfin herb	Lythraceae	Prayer plant	Marantaceae
False heather	Lythraceae	Purple false eranthemum	Acanthaceae
Firecracker flower	Acanthaceae	Purple heart	Commelinaceae
Firecracker plant	Lythraceae	Purple waffle	Acanthaceae
Freckle-face	Acanthaceae	Red Abyssinian banana	Musaceae
Giant taro	Araceae	Red hot cat's tail	Euphorbiaceae
Glorybower	Verbenaceae	Red ivy	Acanthaceae
Glory bush	Melastomataceae	Rose bay	Apocynaceae
Golden candle	Acanthaceae	Rubber plant	Moraceae
Golden dewdrop	Verbenaceae	Ruellia	Acanthaceae
Golden pothos	Araceae	Sage	Verbenaceae
Hawaiian hibiscus	Malvaceae	Sago palm	Cycadaceae
Indoor clover	Amaranthaceae	Screw pine	Pandanaceae
Jacob's coat	Euphorbiaceae	Shrimp plant	Acanthaceae
Jellie peperomia	Piperaceae	Shrub verbena	Verbenaceae
Joseph's coat	Amaranthaceae	Silver-leafed plectranthus	Labiatae
Jungle geranium	Rubiaceae	Snakeplant	Agavaceae
Licorice plant	Compositae	Snowbush	Euphorbiaceae
Lollipop plant	Acanthaceae	Song of India	Agavaceae
Majesty palm	Palmae	Spider plant	Liliaceae
Mandevilla	Apocynaceae	Spineless yucca	Agavaceae
Maroon-leaved hibiscus	Malvaceae	Sweet potato	Convolvulaceae
Mediterranean fan palm	Palmae	Taro	Araceae
Mexican flamevine	Compositae	Ti plant	Agavaceae
Moses-in-the-boat	Commelinaceae	Tricolor dracaena	Agavaceae
Mother-in-law's tongue	Agavaceae	Umbrella plant	Cyperaceae
New Zealand flax	Agavaceae	Variegated crepe ginger	Zingiberaceae
Oleander	Apocynaceae	Variegated flowering maple	Malvaceae
Orange jasmine	Rutaceae	Variegated pineapple	Bromeliaceae
Orange jessamine	Rutaceae	Variegated plectranthus	Labiatae
Oyster plant	Commelinaceae	Variegated shell ginger	Zingiberaceae
Paper flower	Nyctaginaceae	Variegated tapioca	Euphorbiaceae
Parrot leaf	Amaranthaceae	Wandering jew	Commelinaceae
Passion flower vine	Passifloraceae	White butterfly ginger	Zingiberaceae
Peregrina	Euphorbiaceae	Yellow mandevilla	Apocynaceae
		Zebra plant	Acanthaceae

ACANTHACEAE

Aphelandra squarrosa
(Zebra plant)

Origin: Brazil

Decorative interest: This small shrub is grown for its beautiful silvery-white variegated foliage. Large oval leaves with sunken veins, about 8 in. long and 4 in. wide, are arranged opposite each other on the stem. A 6-in. floral spike, composed of yellow flowers emerging from long-lasting yellow bracts, is produced at the top of the stem.

Culture: Light shade, moist soil, warm nights.

Height: 6 in. to 18 in.

Propagation: Stem cuttings in spring.

Horticultural use: Use the zebra plant in the foreground of a border or in a container. In a lightly shaded container, combine it with *Sansevieria trifasciata* 'Laurentii', *Dracaena reflexa* 'Song of India', *Chlorophytum comosum* 'Vittatum', or *Helichrysum petiolare* 'Limelight'.

Overwintering: Purchase new 6-in. flowering pots, which generally contain three rooted cuttings, in May. They are common houseplants in garden centers.

Barleria cristata
(Philippine violet)

Origin: India, Burma

Decorative interest: This small shrub is grown for its 1-in.- to 2-in.-wide blue-violet

---

flowers, which appear sporadically throughout the summer and usually about one month after shearing. Elliptic green leaves, 1 in. to 4 in. long, are opposite.

Culture: Full sun to light shade, normal water; drier soil encourages flowering. Prune into topiary or hedge forms (which also encourages flowering).

Height: 1 ft. to 4 ft.

Propagation: Stem cuttings in spring or summer.

Horticultural use: Grow into a standard for containers. Underplant with *Tradescantia pallida* 'Purple Heart' or *Tradescantia zebrina*. Or plant in the foreground of a border near bronze or burgundy foliage, like *Pseuderanthemum atropurpureum* or *Strobilanthes dyerianus*, which highlights flower color.

Overwintering: Root cuttings in summer and grow as a houseplant for next year's display. Dig, pot, and bring plants indoors to a warm, sunny windowsill about October 1, where they are successful flowering houseplants. Or try to purchase new plants in May. Florida-grown plants are occasionally found in garden centers.

Crossandra infundibuliformis
(syn. *C. undulifolia*)
(Firecracker flower)

Origin: Southern India, Sri Lanka

Decorative interest: Greenhouse-grown pots appear herbaceous, but this plant is actually a small shrub. Salmon-pink to orange flowers, 1 in. to 2 in., are borne on 6-in. spikes. Glossy green, lance-shaped

---

leaves, 2 in. to 5 in. long and 2 in. wide, are arranged opposite each other on the stem.

Culture: Full sun, normal water, warm night temperatures.

Height: 6 in. to 2 ft.

Propagation: Stem cuttings in spring or summer.

Horticultural use: Position this plant in the foreground of a border or in a container. Combine with the russet foliage color of *Acalypha godseffiana* 'Heterophylla' or salmon-flowered *Hibiscus rosa-sinensis*.

Overwintering: Root cuttings in summer and grow as a houseplant for next year's display. Dig, pot, and bring plants indoors to a warm, sunny windowsill about October 1, where they are successful flowering houseplants. Or purchase new plants in May. Four-inch, Florida-grown flowering plants are common in the houseplant section of garden centers or home stores.

Graptophyllum pictum
(syn. *G. hortense*)
(Caricature plant)

Origin: Southeast Asia, New Guinea

Decorative interest: This choice shrub is grown for its 4-in. to 6-in. bronze and assorted variegated leaf colors. The foliage of one clone has a creamy-pink leaf center with reddish-bronze margin (top photo facing page), while that of a different clone has a pink center and a cream margin. Related species have golden or gray variegated leaves. Small flower spikes with clusters of tubular, crimson-purple flowers are rarely produced in zone 6 (or below) gardens.

Culture: Full sun for best foliage color but tolerates shade. Moist organic soil but tolerates drier soil. Warm night temperatures. Pinch plants to keep bushy. Prune second-year plants 8 in. to 12 in. tall in spring.

Height: To 5 ft.

Propagation: Easy from stem cuttings at any season.

Horticultural use: Position young plants in the foreground and 2-year-old plants in the middle of borders. Combine large plants with the bronze-streaked banana *Musa sumatrana* or other bronze and variegated plants. Try it near salmon-flowered *Hibiscus rosa-sinensis*, canna cultivars, or pink New Guinea impatiens.

Overwintering: Root cuttings in summer and grow as a houseplant for next year's display. To achieve large specimens, dig, pot, and bring plants indoors about October 1 to a warm, sunny plant room, greenhouse, or windowsill, where they are successful houseplants.

Hemigraphis alternata
(syn. *H. colorta*)
(Purple waffle, red ivy)

Origin: India, Java

Decorative interest: The purple waffle takes its name from its foliage color—upper surfaces are purplish gray, under surfaces are deep burgundy—and its venation. Sunken veins provide the leaf with a waffle-like appearance. Oval to heart-shaped leaves, 3 in. long and 2 in. wide, are arranged opposite each other on the stem. Their edges are toothed. Small, white flowers, ½ in. to ¾ in., are borne on a terminal spike.

Culture: Full sun to light shade, normal water, tolerates drier soil.

Height: 6 in. to 1 ft.

Propagation: Easy from stem cuttings at any time of year. Cuttings taken in April form full-size plants in one growing season.

Horticultural use: This plant can be grown as a ground cover in the foreground of a border. It will also cascade down the sides of a container or hanging basket. Underplant the large leaves of *Colocasia* 'Black Magic' with the purple waffle or contrast its small purple leaf with the stiff and upright form of *Tradescantia spathacea*. Their colors harmonize. Combine these foliages with the reddish-purple flowers of *Cuphea hyssopifolia*.

Overwintering: Root stem cuttings in September, then grow as a houseplant on a warm, sunny windowsill for next year's display. Or purchase new 4-in. pots or hanging baskets at garden centers in spring.

Hypoestes phyllostachya
(syn. *H. sanguinolenta*)
(Polka-dot plant, freckle-face)

Origin: Madagascar

Decorative interest: Like *Graptophyllum*, *Pseuderanthemum*, and *Sanchezia*, this acanth is grown for its foliage. The common names allude to the white, pink, or rose-colored speckles that occur on top of paired green or bronzy-green oval leaves, about 2 in. long, with slender petioles about two-thirds that length. *Hypoestes phyllostachya* 'Pink Splash' has large pink spots (photo at right). Small lavender-blue flowers occur at the top of stems but are not the ornamental feature.

Culture: Partial to full sun, moist, well-drained soil. Avoid hot, midday summer sun. Pinch to keep bushy.

Height: 1 ft. to 2 ft.

Propagation: Seed or stem cuttings at any season. Cuttings taken in April form full-size plants in one growing season.

Horticultural use: In the foreground of sunny borders combine pink polka-dot plants with pink flowers, like *Justicia carnea* and the ruby-bronze leaves of *Alternanthera dentata* 'Rubiginosa'. In dappled shade they nicely spice pink impatiens. Add pink caladium leaves to the composition. White-spotted *Hypoestes* combine well with the green and white caladium cultivar 'Candidum' and the white-flowered cat's whiskers (*Orthosiphon stamineus*). Use them with other green and white variegated foliage like *Tradescantia fluminensis* 'Albovittata'. These combinations are also effective in containers.

Overwintering: Root stem cuttings in summer, then grow as a houseplant on an east or west windowsill for next year's display. Or prune, dig, pot, and bring *Hypoestes* to an east or west windowsill about October 1 and grow as a stock plant. Root cuttings in March and April for summer use. Or purchase new plants in May. Most nurseries and garden centers now sell them with their bedding plants.

Justicia brandegeana
(syn. *Beloperone guttata*)
(Shrimp plant)

Origin: Mexico

Decorative interest: This plant appears herbaceous, but it is actually a small shrub

that is grown for its drooping, shrimplike flower spikes, 4 in. to 5 in. long, which are composed of 1-in. heart-shaped coppery-pink bracts. The cultivar *J.* 'Yellow Queen' has chartreuse-yellow bracts. White flowers, 2 in. long, protrude from the bracts of both plants, which are ornamental long after the flowers finish. Oval leaves, 1 in. to 3 in. long, are arranged opposite each other on the stem.

Culture: Full sun, normal water, tolerates drier soil.

Height: 6 in. to 2 ft.

Propagation: Stem cuttings in spring and summer.

Horticultural use: Use in the foreground of borders or the middle of containers so that the bases of the exposed stems are hidden. Prune plants that become too leggy. Combine with *Acalypha wilkesiana*, coleus, or canna that have foliage and flower colors similar to the bract color of the shrimp plant. Combine *J.* 'Yellow Queen' with chartreuse or yellow variegated foliage, like *Ipomoea batatus* 'Margarita' or *Canna* 'Pretoria'.

Overwintering: Root stem cuttings in summer, then grow as a houseplant on a warm, sunny windowsill for next year's display. Monitor for whitefly. Or purchase new 4-in. or 6-in. pots at garden centers or specialty nurseries in spring.

Justicia carnea
(syn. *Jacobinia carnea*)
(Brazilian plume)

Origin: Northern South America

Decorative interest: Grow this plant for its spectacular 4-in.- to 6-in.-long flower spike, which is composed of numerous 1-in. to 2-in. rosy-pink flowers that top stems. Small, shrubby plants flower about three times during a zone 6 growing season. Glossy green, broad oval leaves, 6 in. long and 2½ in. wide, are deeply veined and arranged opposite each other on the stem.

Culture: Full sun, normal water.

Height: 6 in. to 2 ft.

Propagation: Stem cuttings in spring and summer.

Horticultural use: Position the Brazilian plume in the foreground of a border. Combine it with the rosy-pink foliage of *Iresine herbstii* and caladium or the bronze foliage of *Alternanthera dentata* 'Rubiginosa'.

Overwintering: Root stem cuttings in summer, then grow as a houseplant on a sunny windowsill for next year's display. Or dig, pot, and bring plants indoors to a warm, sunny windowsill or plant room about October 1. Or purchase new 4-in. or 6-in. pots at garden centers or specialty nurseries in May.

Pachystachys lutea
(Golden candle, lollipop plant)

Origin: Peru

Decorative interest: This plant appears herbaceous but is a small shrub. It is grown for erect 4-in. to 6-in. flower spikes composed of upright, heart-shaped, golden yellow bracts, from which white flowers protrude. Bracts remain ornamental long after flowers finish. Rich green lance-shaped leaves, 6 in. long, are arranged opposite each other on the stem.

Culture: Full sun, normal water.

Height: 6 in. to 2 ft.

Propagation: Stem cuttings in spring and summer.

Horticultural use: Position the golden candle in the foreground of a border or use in containers. Combine with golden-flowered *Lantana camara* or variegated foliage like *Sanchezia speciosa*.

Overwintering: Root stem cuttings in summer, then grow as a houseplant on a sunny windowsill for next year's display. Or dig, pot, and bring plants indoors to a warm, sunny windowsill or plant room about October 1. Monitor for whitefly. Or purchase new 4-in. or 6-in. pots at garden centers or specialty nurseries in May.

Pseuderanthemum atropurpureum
(syn. *Eranthemum atropurpureum*)
(Purple false eranthemum)

Origin: Polynesia

Decorative interest: One of the best bronze-foliaged small shrubs. Opposite, elliptic, glossy leaves, 4 in. to 6 in. long and 2 in. wide, are rich purplish-bronze; sometimes leaves of *Pseuderanthemum atropurpureum* 'Tricolor' are marked with streaks of pink, white, or cream. Several cultivars exist, and their nomenclature is confused. A white-and-green variegated clone exists. Mature plants produce 6-in. green flower spikes, from which emerge 1-in.-long white tubular flowers (but rarely in zone 6 or below gardens).

Culture: Full sun, normal water, warm night temperatures. Tolerates light shade and drier soil.

Height: To 5 ft.

Propagation: Easy from stem cuttings at any season.

Horticultural use: Position young plants in the foreground of borders and older plants in the middle, or use in containers. Combine with the pinky-white variegated foliage of *Breynia nivosa* 'Roseapicta', the blue-violet flowers of *Barleria cristata*, or the red flowers of *Pentas lanceolata, Jatropha integerrima*, and *Ruellia graecizans*.

Overwintering: Root cuttings in summer and grow as a houseplant in bright light for next year's display. To achieve large specimens, dig, pot, and bring plants indoors in late summer to a sunny plant room, greenhouse, or windowsill, where they are successful houseplants. Temperatures below 50°F may blacken leaves. Prune leggy plants back in spring or summer. Or order new plants from specialty houseplant catalogs.

Ruellia graecizans
(syn. *R. amoena*)

Origin: South America

Decorative interest: This neatly domed, subshrub is grown for its tubular red flowers, about 1 in. long, that are freely produced throughout the growing season. Elliptic leaves, about 2 in. long, are paired.

Culture: Full sun, normal water, moist well-drained soil.

Height: 18 in. to 36 in.

Propagation: Stem cuttings or seed. Plants self-seed freely in the garden.

Horticultural use: Position in the foreground of a border with red *Pentas lanceo-*

lata and burgundy foliage like *Pseuderanthemum atropurpureum* and *Iresine herbstii*.

Overwintering: Root stem cuttings in summer, then grow as a houseplant on a sunny windowsill for next year's display. Or dig, pot, and bring parent plants or seedlings indoors to a sunny windowsill or plant room about October 1. Prune back. Monitor for spider mite.

Sanchezia speciosa
(syn. *S. nobilis, S. glaucophylla, S. spectabilis*)

Origin: Ecuador, Peru

Decorative interest: This fast-growing plant is one of my favorites, grown for its large, bold-textured leaves that are arranged opposite each other on the stem. Broad oval leaves, 9 in. to 12 in. long and 3 in. to 4 in. wide, are dark green with strong yellow stripes along the midrib and veins. Two-in.-long tubular yellow flowers, produced on flower spikes, are a bonus on mature shrubby plants (but not common in zone 6 or below gardens).

Culture: Full sun to light shade, normal water, warm night temperatures.

Height: 1 ft. to 4 ft.

Propagation: Easy from stem cuttings at any season. Cuttings taken April 1 form 3-ft. to 4-ft. plants in one growing season.

Horticultural use: Position young plants in the middle and 2-year-old plants in the rear of borders. Combine with other golden variegated plants like *Alpinia zerumbet* 'Variegata' and yellow flowers like *Allamanda* or *Pachystachys lutea*.

Overwintering: Root cuttings in summer and grow as a houseplant on a warm, sunny windowsill for next year's display. To achieve large, 6-ft. specimens, dig, pot, and bring plants indoors about October 1 to a warm, sunny, and humid plant room or greenhouse. Prune back in spring or summer when leggy. Or purchase new plants in May from specialty garden centers and nurseries.

Strobilanthes dyerianus
(Persian shield)

Origin: Burma

Decorative interest: Splendid, pointed oval leaves, 6 in. long and 2 in. wide, are arranged opposite each other on the stem. Upper surfaces are dark green with a glimmering metallic-blue sheen; under surfaces are deep purple. Old leaves fade in full sun, new leaves shimmer. This small, shrubby plant is generally not grown for the funnel-shaped, pale blue flowers, 1½ in. long, that form on spikes within leaf axils during short-day conditions.

Culture: Full sun to light shade, moist soil.

Height: 6 in. to 4 ft.

Propagation: Stem cutting in spring and summer.

Horticultural use: Use this choice plant in the foreground to middle of borders or in containers. Combine with purple or lavender flowers like heliotrope or *Lantana montevidensis* or purple foliage like *Tradescantia pallida* 'Purple Heart', *Tradescantia spathacea*, and *Hemigraphis alternata*.

Overwintering: Root cuttings in summer and grow as a houseplant on a warm, sunny windowsill for next year's display. Dig, pot, and bring plants into a 65°F greenhouse about October 1 to use as stock plants. Monitor for aphids. Or purchase new plants from specialty garden centers in May.

Thunbergia alata
(Black-eyed Susan vine)

Origin: Tropical Africa

Decorative interest: Fast-growing vine producing 2-in.-wide flowers that range in color from bright orange to pale yellow or white and have a central brown eye. Triangular-shaped, green leaves, 3 in. long and 3 in. wide, are arranged opposite each other on stems.

Culture: Full sun, normal water. Prune excess growth when necessary.

Height: To 8 ft.

Propagation: Sow seed indoors four weeks before planting outdoors or sow directly outdoors in early May.

Horticultural use: Cover a trellis or other vine support or grow in a hanging basket. As a pendulous plant in a hanging basket or container, mix with *Ipomoea batatus* 'Blackie'.

Overwintering: Purchase new seed each spring.

Thunbergia grandiflora
(Blue trumpet vine)

Origin: Northern India

Decorative interest: This vigorous vine is slower than *Thunbergia alata* in zone 6 gardens but produces beautiful flaring, 5-in., pale blue trumpet-shaped flowers. A white cultivar, *Thunbergia grandiflora* 'Alba', exists. Dark-green, 8-in., heart-shaped leaves are attractive and arranged opposite each other along the stems.

Culture: Full sun, normal water.

Height: To 6 ft.

Propagation: Stem cutting in spring.

Horticultural use: Grow on a trellis or other vine support. Combine with *Passiflora caerulea*.

Overwintering: Dig, pot, and bring plants into a 65°F plant room or greenhouse about October 1. Or purchase new Florida- or California-grown container plants in garden centers in May.

AGAVACEAE

Agave americana
(syn. *A. altissima*)
(Century plant, American aloe)

Origin: Eastern Mexico

Decorative interest: This open-rosetted succulent is an architectural foliage plant, grown for its stiff, linear, blue-green leaves, 1 ft. to 3 ft. long and 3 in. wide (though they can reach 6 ft.). Leaves are edged with spines and tipped with a sharp, brown 2-in. needle. Leaves of the cultivar *A.* 'Marginata' have yellow margins; those of *A.* 'Mediopicta' (photo above) have a central yellow band. Flower spikes, up to 20 ft. tall, are unlikely to appear in temperate gardens.

Culture: Full sun, well-drained soil, drought tolerant. Tolerates hot to cool temperatures.

Height: 1 ft. to 4 ft.

Propagation: Divide basal pups.

Horticultural use: Architectural plant for specimen use in Grecian-style containers.

Overwintering: Place parent plant or pups into a cold but frost-free garage or basement, preferably with some light. Water monthly. Prune away old leaves in spring.

Cordyline indivisa
(syn. *Dracaena indivisa*)
(Cabbage palm)

Origin: New Zealand

Decorative interest: This is an architectural foliage plant grown for the rosette of stiff,

sword-shaped leaves, up to 3 ft. long and 3 in. wide, that whorl around the top of erect, single-trunk spikes. It is not grown for flowers. The related and similar *Cordyline australis* 'Purple Tower' (photo above) is bronze shaded, and *Cordyline australis* 'Aureo-striata' is striped yellow. *Cordyline indivisa* is confused with *Cordyline australis*, which differs by having a stout red and white midrib. *Cordyline* differs from *Dracaena* by the number of ovules in each cell of the ovary; one in *Dracaena*, several in *Cordyline*.

Culture: Sun, normal water, tolerates drier conditions.

Height: Up to 6 ft.

Propagation: Seed, stem cuttings, or air layer.

Horticultural use: Cordyline is an architectural plant for the center of a Victorian cast-iron container with red geraniums, petunias, pendulous *Tradescantia zebrina*, or *Chlorophytum comosum* 'Vittatum'. Or use in the center of a Victorian-style lawn bed with *Canna* 'The President', *Salvia splendens,* and silver dusty miller. Create a carpet bed with ribbons of *Iresine herbstii* and *Alternanthera ficoidea.*

Overwintering: Purchase new plants, which are common and inexpensive in garden centers, in May. Or place plants into a cold but frost-free garage or basement, preferably with some light. Water monthly. Acclimate to sunshine in April. If left outdoors. they remain green and attractive for much of the winter, despite their frozen death.

Cordyline terminalis (syn. *C. fruticosa*) (Ti plant)

Origin: Southeast Asia, Hawaii

Decorative interest: This is a foliage plant grown for the rosette of lance-shaped leaves, about 12 in. long and 3 in. wide, that whorl around the top of erect, single-trunk spikes. Dozens of cultivars with leaves in various shades of cream, crimson, copper, pink, and purple exist. Not grown for flowers.

Culture: Light shade, normal water, high humidity. Intolerant of drought. Warm night temperatures. Monitor for spider mite.

Height: 1 ft. to 3 ft.

Propagation: Stem cuttings or air layer.

Horticultural use: Architectural plant for the center of a container. Combine with a vigorous fuchsia like *F.* 'Mrs. J. D. Fredericks', the pink-flowered *Justicia carnea*, or *Mandevilla sanderi* 'Rosea', or grow the viny *Mandevilla* x *amoena* 'Alice du Pont' up its stems. Foliage color is similar to that of *Iresine herbstii* 'Brilliantissima'.

Overwintering: Purchase new plants, which are common in the houseplant section of garden centers, in May. Ti plants are prone to spider mites when they are grown as a houseplant.

Dracaena marginata 'Tricolor' (Tricolor dracaena)

Origin: Obscure

Decorative interest: This is a good architectural foliage plant that is grown for the

rosette of 1-ft.- to 2-ft.-long and ½-in.-wide sword-shaped leaves. They whorl around the top of bare single-trunk stems that often whimsically bend and twist. They are striped pink, cream, and green. A larger, more vigorous clone, *D.m.* 'Bicolor' (photo above), has less red variegation. Growth is slower than *Cordyline indivisa*.

Culture: Acclimate to full sun or light shade, normal water.

Height: 6 in. to 6 ft.

Propagation: Stem cuttings or air layer.

Horticultural use: Place this architectural plant in the center of a container. Combine with *Acalypha godseffiana* 'Heterophylla'. Or use green and white forms as a border focal point near bronze foliage like *Alternanthera dentata* 'Rubiginosa' or variegated foliage like *Hibiscus rosa-sinensis* 'Cooperi'. Underplant with *Tradescantia fluminensis* 'Albovittata'.

Overwintering: Dig, pot, and bring plants indoors to grow as a houseplant on a bright windowsill or a 65°F plant room about October 1. Or purchase new plants in May. Six-inch pots with three rooted cuttings and larger specimens are common in the houseplant section of garden centers and flower shops.

Dracaena reflexa 'Song of India' (syn. *Pleomele reflexa* 'Song of India') (Song of India)

Origin: Madagascar

Decorative interest: Song of India is grown for its variegated leaves with creamy yellow margin, about 5 in. long and 1 in. wide, which tightly whorl around stems. Young single-trunk spikes are slow growing and branch as they age.

Culture: Light shade, acclimate to full sun, normal water, tolerates drier conditions.

Height: 6 in. to 3 ft.

Propagation: Stem cuttings or air layer.

Horticultural use: Use in a lightly shaded container with *Sansevieria trifasciata* 'Laurentii', *Aphelandra squarrosa,* and *Chlorophytum comosum* 'Vittatum'.

Overwintering: Dig, pot, and bring plants indoors to grow as a choice houseplant on a bright windowsill or a 65°F plant room about October 1. Or purchase new plants in May. Six-inch pots with three rooted cuttings and larger specimens are common in the houseplant section of garden centers and flower shops.

Furcraea foetida 'Mediopicta' (syn. *F. foetida* 'Variegata', *F. gigantia* 'Mediopicta')

Origin: West Indies

Decorative interest: The succulent rosetted spearlike leaves provide an architectural effect similar to *Agave americana* but more hemispherical and with fewer spines. Its variegation is splendid. Ice-cream-color stripes, French vanilla and mint green, illuminate stiff leaves, 5 in. wide and 3 ft. long.

Culture: Full sun, well-drained soil, drought tolerant.

Height: 1 ft. to 4 ft.

Propagation: Plantlets form freely on flowering stems but rarely in temperate gardens.

Horticultural use: Choice architectural plant for specimen use in containers. Contrast with cascading burgundy foliage like *Ipomoea batatus* 'Blackie'.

Overwintering: Dig, pot, and bring plants indoors about October 1 to grow as a houseplant on a sunny windowsill, in a plant room or greenhouse at about 55°F to 60°F night temperatures. Water sparingly.

Phormium tenax (New Zealand flax)

Origin: New Zealand

Decorative interest: This handsome architectural foliage plant forms a herbaceous clump of long, fastigiate, sword-shaped leaves that range in color from glaucous green to bronze. Cultivars with bronze foliage include 'Purpureum' and 'Bronze Baby', which is shorter (2 ft. to 3 ft.). Variegations of cream and green (*P. tenax* 'Variegatum', photo below) and red, pink, and yellow (*P. tenax* 'Aurora') exist.

P. colensoi (syn. *P. cookianum*) is a similar but slightly shorter species.

Culture: Sun or light shade, normal water. Plants tolerate slightly moist or slightly dry soil but are best in cool, moist conditions. In hot, dry conditions monitor for spider mite. Apply a slow-release fertilizer at planting.

Height: 2 ft. to 6 ft., depending on cultivar.

Propagation: Division of rhizomes, but wait until specimens are at least 3 years old.

Horticultural use: Position this architectural plant in the center of a container planting or Victorian-style lawn bed, or as a focal plant in a border. Combine bronze-leaved forms with other bronze-foliaged plants like *Alternanthera dentata* 'Rubiginosa' and *Pseuderanthemum atropurpureum,* or tricolored foliage like *Hibiscus rosa-sinensis* 'Cooperi'. Cream variegated forms combine well with chartreuse foliage like *Helichrysum petiolare* 'Limelight'. Use as punctuation in the center of lawn beds of *Alternanthera ficoidea, Iresine herbstii,* or waxed begonias.

Overwintering: To achieve large specimen plants, dig, pot, and bring plants into a cold but frost-free garage or basement, preferably with some light, about November 1. Water monthly. Acclimate to sunshine in April. They can be planted outdoors in late April or early May when nights are still cool. Or bring indoors and grow as a houseplant on a cool, bright windowsill, in a plant room, or greenhouse. Specimen plants do not form the first season after division, and they are not commonly available in nurseries or garden centers in the Northeast. Search them out in specialty nurseries. Three-year-old plants are best.

Sansevieria trifasciata 'Laurentii' (Mother-in-law's tongue, snakeplant)

Origin: Nigeria

Decorative interest: Clumps of erect and stiff, sword-shaped marbled leaves are edged in golden yellow. Plants generally are not grown for the sporadic and curious erect flower spikes, about 12 in. tall with small, six-petaled white flowers.

Culture: Shade or acclimate to full sun. Normal water but tolerates drier soil.

Height: To 4 ft.

Propagation: Division of rhizomes.

Horticultural use: Use this architectural plant for its strong fastigiate form in containers or borders. Combine with other golden variegated plants like *Sanchezia speciosa* or chartreuse-foliaged *Helichrysum petiolare* 'Limelight', *Ipomoea batatus* 'Margarita', and coleus cultivars.

Overwintering: Dig, pot, and bring plants indoors to grow as an easy, pest-free houseplant about October 1. Or purchase new plants in May. Sansevieria is common and inexpensive in garden centers and home stores.

Yucca elephantipes 'Variegata' (syn. *Y. guatamalensis*) (Spineless yucca)

Origin: Mexico, Central America

Decorative interest: This architectural plant grows as a basal rosette or a single-trunked spike of rosetted, sword-shaped leaves, 1 ft. to 4 ft. long and 1 in. to 3 in. wide. Creamy white stripes highlight the margin of each leaf. *Yucca aloifolia* 'Tricolor' is similar but with a central white stripe. Mature plants produce a 2-ft.-tall flower spike from the center of the rosette with many white, six-petaled, 3-in.-long, bell-shaped flowers. However, the flower is not common in zone 6 gardens (and below).

Culture: Full sun, tolerant of drier soil.

Height: 1 ft. to 4 ft.

Propagation: Stem cuttings or air layer.

Horticultural use: Position this architectural plant in the center of containers and Victorian-style lawn beds or as a focal plant in borders. In containers, combine with the pendulous or ground-covering chartreuse foliage of *Ipomoea batatus* 'Margarita' or

contrast it against the dark foliage of *Ipomoea batatus* 'Blackie'. Ring ribbons of various leaf shades of *Alternanthera ficoidea*, *Iresine herbstii*, or coleus around it in Victorian-style lawn beds.

Overwintering: Dig, pot, and bring plants into a cold but frost-free garage or basement, preferably with some light, about November 1. Water monthly. Acclimate to sunshine in April. Or bring indoors as a houseplant in a sunny window, plant room, or greenhouse. Or purchase new plants in May. They are widely available in garden centers and home stores as indoor foliage plants and are inexpensive. Six-inch pots with two or three plants can be divided into individual specimens.

AMARANTHACEAE

Alternanthera dentata 'Rubiginosa' (Indoor clover)

Origin: West Indies

Decorative interest: Deep, burgundy-red leaves, about 3 in. long and 1½ in. wide, are arranged alternately along the stem. They are rich and fresh throughout the growing season (unlike some burgundy-red leaves that lose their color). Plants appear herbaceous but are actually weak-stemmed shrubs.

Culture: Sun for best foliage color, normal water. Vigorous plants require pruning to keep under control.

Height: To 3 ft.

Propagation: Easy from stem cuttings.

Horticultural use: Position in the middle of a border near the pendulous reddish flowers of *Acalypha hispida* or *Amaranthus caudatus* or underplant large, bronze variegated bananas like *Musa sumatrana* and *Ensete ventricosum* 'Maurelii'. Use it to intensify the the fluorescent orange of *Cosmos sulphureus*, *Zinnia angustifolia*, or *Lantana camara* 'Radiation'.

Overwintering: Root stem cuttings in September and overwinter on a sunny windowsill. Plants produce white cloverlike flowers (hence the common name) during the short days of winter, which halts growth until longer days return. Or purchase new plants at garden centers in May.

Alternanthera ficoidea (Parrot leaf, Joseph's coat)

Origin: Brazil

Decorative interest: This spreading, low, bushy ground cover is a foliage plant. Oval to linear leaves, 1 in. to 2 in. long, are

arranged alternately in shades of bronze, red, pink, yellow, or green. Numerous forms and cultivars exist. *A. ficoidea* 'Amoena' (photo bottom right, p. 137) is mottled red, pink, orange, and bronze; *A. ficoidea* 'Aurea' is yellow or chartreuse; and *A. ficoidea* 'Purpurea' is burgundy. Bristly white flowers are insignificant.

Culture: Full sun, normal water, easy to grow. Clip to form tight and bushy plants. Thrives in hot, humid conditions.

Height: 6 in. to 1 ft.

Propagation: Easy from stem cuttings in any media at any season. Like coleus, they even root in water.

Horticultural use: This historic plant is the standard for Victorian carpet beds. Ribbons of different-colored and different-textured leaf forms, in combination with dusty miller and coleus, traditionally surround spikes of *Cordyline indivisa* in circular lawn beds. Ring them around *Phormium tenax, Yucca elephantipes, Colocasia esculenta, Canna* x *generalis,* or *Ricinus communis.* They are also good container plants.

Overwintering: Root stem cuttings in September to overwinter on a sunny windowsill.

Iresine herbstii
(Beefsteak plant, blood leaf, chicken gizzard)

Origin: Brazil

Decorative interest: This spreading, low, bushy ground cover is grown as a foliage plant. Oval leaves, 2 in. long, are arranged alternately on the stem in shades of bronze, red, pink, yellow, and green. *I. herbstii* 'Brilliantissima' has rich carmine-crimson colored leaves and stems. *I. herbstii*

'Aureoriticulata' (photo bottom left) has golden venation and reddish petioles. Bristly white flowers are insignificant.

Culture: Full sun, normal water, tolerates drier soil. Pinch to form tight and bushy plants. Thrives in hot, humid conditions.

Height: 1 ft. to 2 ft.

Propagation: Easy from stem cuttings.

Horticultural use: This is another Victorian carpet bedding plant to be used like (and with) *Alternanthera ficoidea.*

Overwintering: Root stem cuttings in September to overwinter on a sunny windowsill.

APOCYNACEAE

Allamanda cathartica
(Common allamanda)

Origin: Tropical South America

Decorative interest: This loose, viny shrub is grown for its clear, bright yellow, five-petaled, funnel-shaped flowers that are 3 in. to 4 in. wide. The cultivar *A. cathartica* 'Grandiflora' has large clear yellow flowers over 4 in. in diameter. Glossy, dark green leaves, 4 in. to 6 in. long and 1 in. to 2 in. wide, whorl around the stems.

Culture: Full sun, moist, well-drained soil, warm temperature, high humidity. Warm night temperatures. Pinch to encourage a bushy habit, then root the cuttings.

Height: 3 ft. to 6 ft.

Propagation: Stem cuttings in spring or summer.

Horticultural use: Position in the middle of a border, either staked or on a vine support, near golden-foliaged and variegated plants like *Sanchezia speciosa* or *Alpinia zerumbet* 'Variegata'. Let them ramble into banana plants for support.

Overwintering: Dig, pot, and bring *Allamanda* into a sunny, warm (60°F), and humid plant room or greenhouse in mid-September. It can be difficult to grow as a houseplant. Keep almost dry in winter. Or purchase new Florida-grown plants in 5-gal. pots from specialty garden centers in May.

Allamanda schottii
(syn. *A. nerifolia*)
(Bush allamanda)

Origin: Tropical South America

Decorative interest: This is a smaller, shrubbier, and more floriferous plant than *Allamanda cathartica*, with smaller, five-petaled, funnel-shaped flowers, about 2 in. in diameter, that are still clear, deep yellow, and beautiful. Glossy, dark green leaves, about 4 in. long and 1 in. to 2 in. wide, whorl around stems.

Culture: Full sun, moist, well-drained soil, high humidity. Warm night temperatures.

Height: 18 in. to 4 ft.

Propagation: Stem cuttings in spring or summer.

Horticultural use: Position in the foreground of a border near other golden-foliaged and variegated plants like *Sanchezia speciosa* or *Alpinia zerumbet* 'Variegata', or burgundy foliage like *Pseuderanthemum atropurpureum.* Combine with other yellow flowers like *Pachystachys lutea. A. schottii* is

a better border plant than *A. cathartica* that's easier to grow in zone 6 gardens and is usually cheaper in garden centers. It is always in flower.

Overwintering: Root cuttings in summer and grow on a warm, sunny windowsill for next year's display. Dig, pot, and bring *Allamanda* into a sunny, warm, and humid plant room or greenhouse in mid-September. It can be difficult to grow as a houseplant. Or purchase new plants from specialty garden centers and nurseries in May.

Mandevilla x *amoena* 'Alice du Pont' (syn. *M.* x *amabilis* 'Alice du Pont')

Origin: Garden hybrid

Decorative interest: This vigorous, twining vine is grown for its abundant, rose-pink flowers, about 4 in. in diameter. Leathery green, oval leaves, about 3 in. long, are arranged opposite each other on the stem.

Culture: Full sun, normal water.

Height: To 8 ft.

Propagation: Stem cuttings in spring.

Horticultural use: Grow on a trellis or other vine support with *Thunbergia grandiflora*. It is often grown in a container with a tepee vine support or attached to a molded chicken-wire form like a topiary.

Overwintering: Dig, pot, and bring *Mandevilla* into a sunny, warm, and humid plant room or greenhouse in mid-September. Or purchase new plants at garden centers and home stores in May.

Mandevilla splendens 'Rosacea' (syn. *Dipladenia splendens*) (Brazilian jasmine)

Origin: Brazil

Decorative interest: Grow this plant for the bright, rose-pink, funnel-shaped flowers about 2 in. to 3 in. in diameter. This shrubby plant twines less than *Mandevilla* 'Alice du Pont' but has glossy, dark green oval leaves, about 2 in. to 3 in. long, that are paired.

Culture: Full sun, normal water, organic soil.

Height: To 3 ft.

Propagation: Stem cuttings in spring or summer.

Horticultural use: Grow in containers with heliotrope, similar pink New Guinea impatiens, and burgundy-foliaged plants, like *Alternanthera dentata* 'Rubiginosa' or *Iresine herbstii* 'Brilliantissima'. Let *Ipomoea batatus* 'Margarita' cascade over the rim. Position in the foreground of borders.

Overwintering: Root cuttings in summer and grow on a warm, sunny windowsill for next year's display. Dig, pot, and bring *Mandevilla* into a sunny, warm, and humid plant room or greenhouse in mid-September. Or purchase new plants at garden centers in May. They are widely available.

Nerium oleander (Oleander, rose bay)

Origin: Mediterranean to western China

Decorative interest: Oleanders are historic shrubs that are grown for their five-petaled

or double flowers in various shades of pink or white. Some are scented. In full sun, semi-dry conditions they are in continuous bloom. Narrow, rich green, leathery leaves, about 6 in. long and 1 in. wide, whorl around stems in groups of three. *All plant parts are deadly poisonous.*

Culture: Full sun, normal water, tolerant of drier soil. Flowers more frequently as soil slightly dries. Tolerates cold temperatures.

Height: 2 ft. to 6 ft.

Propagation: Stem cuttings in spring or summer.

Horticultural use: Grow as a specimen plant in a container or tub. Combine oleander with pots of bougainvillea or date palms to create a Mediterranean look. Arrange them around a swimming pool.

Overwintering: Bring plants into a cold but frost-free garage or basement, preferably with some light, about November 1. Water monthly. Acclimate to sunshine in April or early May. Prune leggy plants back to 12 in. to 18 in. in spring. Or purchase new Florida- or California-grown plants inexpensively from garden centers in May.

Urechites lutea (Yellow mandevilla)

Origin: Southern Florida to Colombia

Decorative interest: *Urechites lutea* is a viny shrub with twining stems that is grown for clear yellow flowers about 2 in. in diameter. Glossy oval leaves, about 3 in. long, are paired. This plant is occasionally mislabeled as *Mandevilla* 'Yellow'.

Culture: Full sun, moist fertile soil, tolerates drier conditions. Warm night temperatures. Shelter from strong wind.

Height: To 6 ft.

Propagation: Stem cuttings in spring or summer.

Horticultural use: Grow on a tepee in a container or on a vine support. Position in the foreground or middle of borders like *Allamanda cathartica* and let the stems twine through other plants. Combine with the pale blue flowers of *Plumbago auriculata* or with yellow variegated plants like *Sanchezia speciosa*.

Overwintering: Before temperatures drop below 55°F bring containerized plants indoors to a warm, sunny plant room or greenhouse. Keep slightly dry during winter. Root cuttings in summer to overwinter on a windowsill (bear in mind that it takes two years to achieve a specimen-size plant). Or purchase Florida-grown plants from garden centers in May.

ARACEAE

Alocasia macrorrhiza
(Giant taro)

Origin: Sri Lanka, India, Malaysia

Decorative interest: Like most aroids this plant is grown for foliage. From the tops of thick, aboveground rhizomatic stems, 1-ft.- to 3-ft.-tall, pointed, arrow-shaped leaf blades face upward. Petioles join leaf blades at their base. Leaves of *Alocasia macrorrhiza* are glossy, their edges undulate, and their midribs are broad. The leaves of *A. macror-*

rhiza 'Variegata' (photo below) are like fine marble. Large blotches of white intersperse with green, but sometimes the midrib divides the variegation in two; half the leaf is completely white, half completely green. Almost all-white leaves occur. Metallic lead-shaded leaves of *Alocasia plumbea* (syn. *A. macrorrhiza rubra*, *A. indica* 'Metallica') are similar in form but sparkle. *Alocasia* 'Hilo Beauty' is smaller and resembles a large, chartreuse-splotched caladium.

Culture: Partial shade, acclimate to full sun, rich, moist, well-drained soil, warm temperatures, high humidity.

Height: To 6 ft.

Propagation: Suckers or rhizome divisions with dormant buds. Collect resting tubers from the ends of dormant rhizomes.

Horticultural use: Grow in borders for bold textural and tropical effects. Contrast with *Cyperus alternifolius*. Combine *Alocasia macrorrhiza* 'Variegata' with other white and green variegated plants, like *Costus speciosus* 'Variegatus'. Use *A. plumbea* with red hibiscus and *Musa sumatrana*.

Overwintering: Dig, pot, and bring plants indoors to a warm plant room or greenhouse before temperatures drop below 60°F. Withhold water during the winter. Plants require less humidity at this time. In springtime, increase water, humidity, and nutrients. Bring outdoors after night temperatures are above 60°F.

Caladium x *bicolor*
(Caladium)

Origin: Garden hybrid

Decorative interest: These herbaceous plants are grown for their colorful foliage.

Kaleidoscopic arrow-shaped, peltate leaves, are about 10 in. long and 6 in. wide and form a clump. Dozens of variegated variants exist in shades of green, white, red, and pink. 'Miss Muffet' is a choice whitish form with fuchsia speckles.

Culture: This plant is primarily associated with shade, but darker foliage colors survive and flourish in sun. Moist, rich organic soil. Warm night temperatures.

Height: 1 ft. to 2 ft.

Propagation: Division of tubers in spring.

Horticultural use: Underplant standards of red *Hibiscus rosa-sinensis* with red-leaved caladium. In shade, combine white variegated caladium with *Tradescantia fluminensis* 'Albovittata', white, speckled *Hypoestes*, or *Costus speciosus* 'Variegatus'. Use red-leaved varieties ('Freida Hemple') in Victorian-style lawn beds around canna, *Ensete ventricosum* 'Maurelii', or *Cycas revoluta*. Edge them with coleus 'Red Wizard'.

Overwintering: Dig tubers in early November. Pack clean, dry tubers in dry sphagnum or peat moss and store at about 50°F. Plant them in pots indoors in late April or May. Cover pots with plastic to keep humidity levels and temperatures high. Or purchase new tubers or started plants at garden centers in spring. Don't plant them outdoors until night temperatures are 65°F.

Colocasia esculenta
(syn. *C. antiquorum*, *C. esculentum*)
(Elephant's ear, taro, dasheen, eddoe)

Origin: Tropical East Asia

Decorative interest: Outside the tropics, this splendid plant is grown for its huge green leaves, up to 3 ft. long and 2 ft. wide, on top petioles up to 6 ft. tall. The petiole meets the back of the leaf blade in its middle (a condition termed "peltate"), which enables leaves to nod. At least four purplish foliage cultivars with confused nomenclature are available. *C. esculenta* 'Fontanesii', the purple-stem taro up to 6 ft. tall, has a beautiful red-purple petiole. A form of it with a glaucous leaf blade that is puckered between the veins is sometimes called *Colocasia fontanesii* 'Red-stemmed'. Both are stoloniferous. *C. esculenta* 'Illustris' (photo below), the imperial taro or black caladium, is shorter, 1 ft. to 4 ft., and leaves, smooth as taffeta, are marked blue-black between the veins. It is sometimes called *Colocasia antiquorum* 'Illustris'. The darkest and most elegant form, the cranberry taro, is called *Colocasia* 'Jet Bead Wonder' or *Colocasia antiquorum* 'Black Magic'. It is midway in height between *C.* 'Fontanesii' and *C.* 'Illustris', about 3 ft. to 5 ft. tall, with rich red-purple leaves and petioles.

Culture: Full sun or light shade, moist soil conditions. Incorporate water-absorbent gels into the planting hole. Plants prefer mucky soils rich in organic matter. Water regularly. Can be grown as a water or waterside plant. Prune yellowing leaves to the ground.

Height: 3 ft. to 6 ft.

Propagation: Divide underground tubers.

Horticultural use: Use elephant's ears in Victorian-style lawn beds with *Canna* and *Ricinus communis* or in borders with *Cyperus alternifolius*. I mass them in the rear of the border for a bold textural statement. The purplish-foliage cultivars are frequently grown as water plants but are as successful in moist garden soils. Underplant *Colocasia* 'Fontanesii' with *Tradescantia zebrina*. All combine splendidly with *Strobilanthes dyerianus*, *Tradescantia pallida*

'Purple Heart', and *Tradescantia spathacea*. Combine *C.* 'Black Magic' with red flowers.

Overwintering: In zone 6 and above, dig plants in November, wash, and dry tubers. Store them in dry sphagnum, peat moss, or excelsior until April. Pot up tubers. Keep moist and warm. Plant outdoors in May. Tubers are available inexpensively at garden centers and also in grocery stores that sell Caribbean products—dasheen or eddoe. Full-grown plants are now available at some garden centers in May. Purple-stemmed varieties are not tuberous and require potting and indoor overwintering. Monitor *C.* 'Fontanesii' and *C.* 'Illustris' for spider mites. Prune away infected leaves.

Epipremnum aureum
(syn. *Scindapsus aureus*)
(Golden pothos)

Origin: Southeast Asia, Western Pacific

Decorative interest: This popular viny ground cover is grown for its golden variegated, heart-shaped leaves, 3 in. to 12 in.

Culture: Shade or acclimated to full sun, moist soil conditions.

Height: 6 in. to 3 ft.

Propagation: Easy from cuttings.

Horticultural use: Use as a foreground plant in a tropical border, as a vine on a vine support, or as a trailing edge plant in a container. Combine with *Sansevieria trifasciata* 'Laurentii', *Dracaena* 'Song of India', and *Aphelandra squarrosa* in a container in light shade.

Overwintering: Bring indoors as an easy-to-grow houseplant or purchase new plants in May. Every garden center sells them.

ASCLEPIADACEAE

Stephanotis floribunda
(syn. *Stephanotis jasminoides*
(Bridal wreath)

Origin: Madagascar

Decorative interest: *Stephanotis* is an elegant climbing plant that is grown for its very fragrant, waxy white, funnel-shaped flowers formed in clusters on new growth. Flowers are often used as wedding boutonnieres. Thick, glossy, leathery leaves are about 6 in. long.

Culture: Full sun, normal water, good organic soil, high humidity. Avoid root disturbance.

Height: To 6 ft.

Propagation: Stem cuttings in spring, air layer.

Horticultural use: Grow as container plants in terra-cotta pots or Versailles-style tubs and train on a vine tepee or wire wreath. Position pots where the flower fragrance will be highlighted. Combine with pots of oleander.

Overwintering: Bring pots into a warm, sunny, and humid plant room or greenhouse. Water and mist when in active growth. Specimen-size plants are several years old. Or purchase new California- or Florida-grown plants at garden centers in May.

BIGNONIACEAE

Pandorea jasminoides
(syn. *Tecoma jasminoides*)
(Bower of beauty)

Origin: Northeast Australia

Decorative interest: These vines are grown for their glossy, pinnate leaves and showy, funnel-shaped, white flowers, about 2 in. long, streaked pink inside. A variegated cultivar (photo above) exists.

Culture: Full sun, normal water, tolerates drought but water plentifully when in active growth. Plants tolerate temperatures to 40°F and light frost. Prune when leggy.

Height: To 8 ft.

Propagation: Stem cuttings in summer.

Horticultural use: Grow as a container plant on a vine tepee in terra-cotta pots or wooden tubs. Restricting root growth limits vigorous foliar growth and encourages flowering.

Overwintering: Bring *Pandorea jasminoides* containers into a sunny and cool (50°F to 55°F) plant room or greenhouse in mid-October or before hard frost is predicted. Florida- and California-grown plants are widely available in garden centers in May.

Tecomaria capensis
(syn. *Tecoma capensis,*
Bignonia capensis)
(Cape honeysuckle)

Origin: Tanzania, Zaire, northeast Angola, Zambia, Malawi, northern Mozambique

Decorative interest: Grow this loose, viny shrub for its terminal clusters of tubular orange flowers produced periodically throughout spring, summer, and fall. Pinnate leaves have seven to nine leaflets.

Culture: Full sun, normal water, tolerates cooler growing conditions. Prune when leggy. Flowers appear more frequently when the plant is allowed to dry between watering, making it a good choice for container culture. In rich growing conditions, it remains vegetative. Avoid high-nitrogen fertilizers.

Height: 2 ft. to 5 ft.

Propagation: Stem cuttings.

Horticultural use: Place plants in terra-cotta pots on top of the soil in the middle of a border with *Cuphea ignea* 'David Verity' and orange *Lantana camara*. Use it as a support for *Gloriosa superba* or the orange-flowered vine, *Pseudogynoxis chenopodioides*.

Overwintering: Dig and bring into a cool, sunny greenhouse or plant room in late October. Or bring into a cold but frost-free garage or basement, preferably with some light, about November 1. Or purchase new Florida-grown plants in 5-gal. containers from nurseries and garden centers in May.

BROMELIACEAE

Ananas comosus 'Variegatus'
(Variegated pineapple)

Origin: South America

Decorative interest: This bromeliad relative is grown for the rosette of white-margined, spiny linear leaves, 1 ft. to 3 ft. Flowers, followed by a small pineapple fruit, may top 3-ft.-tall stems on plants about 6 years old but are not common in zone 6 gardens. Leaves of *Ananas bracteatus* 'Tricolor' are flushed and edged red-pink.

Culture: Full sun, slightly dry, organic soil.

Height: To 3 ft.

Propagation: Division of basal offshoots.

Horticultural use: Use this architectural plant in the center of a container as a focal point in gardens. Edge the container with *Tradescantia pallida* 'Purple Heart' for contrast.

Overwintering: Grow as an interior houseplant like bromeliads, but with more sunshine. Or purchase new plants in spring. They are usually sold with bromeliads in the houseplant section of garden centers.

CANNACEAE

Canna x *generalis*
(Canna lily)

Origin: Garden hybrid

Decorative interest: Cannas are herbaceous, rhizomatous plants grown for their large leaves (18 in. long and 6 in. wide) and gladiolus-like blossoms (up to 4 in. in diameter). Flowers appear on short spikes at the apex of stems in shades of red, orange, yellow, or pink. Leaf colors are assorted shades of green and bronze; choice cultivars are striped red, pink, or gold. *C.* 'Pretoria' has golden variegated foliage and orange flowers. *C.* 'Phasion' (left photo facing page)

has leaves with warm pink and bronze stripes. It is marketed as "Tropicanna."

Culture: Sun, normal water, any soil (but best in enriched organic soil).

Height: 2 ft. to 8 ft., depending on cultivar and cultural conditions.

Propagation: Division of rhizomes.

Horticultural use: Use in Victorian-style lawn beds with *Ricinus communis, Colocasia esculenta,* and coleus. Encircle *Canna* 'The President' with *Salvia splendens* for a strong, bold display. Combine the golden variegated 'Pretoria' in borders with *Sanchezia speciosa* and *Abutilon pictum* 'Thompsonii'. Or use in the center of containers.

Overwintering: In zone 6 and above, dig plants in November, wash, and dry rhizomes. Pack them in dry sphagnum, peat moss, or excelsior and store at 50°F until April. Pot the rhizomes with a potting media. Keep moist and warm. Plant outdoors in May. Or plant rhizomes directly outdoors into prepared soil in mid-May. Or keep container specimens potted in a frost-free garage. Plants may be winter-hardy in zone 7 and above.

COMMELINACEAE

Tradescantia fluminensis 'Albovittata' (Wandering jew)

Origin: Southeast Brazil

Decorative interest: This spreading groundcover has green-and-white-striped leaves that are 2 in. long and 1 in. wide.

White, three-petaled flowers, ½ in. in diameter, are insignificant.

Culture: Light shade, normal water.

Height: 6 in. to 1 ft.

Propagation: Easy from cuttings.

Horticultural use: Underplant the green and white variegated *Dracaena marginata* 'Bicolor' in a border or along the edge of a container with *Tradescantia fluminensis* 'Albovittata'. In shade, combine with the green and white variegated *Caladium bicolor* 'Candidum' or a white-speckled *Hypoestes.*

Overwintering: Take cuttings in autumn to overwinter as houseplants. Propagate them in spring.

Tradescantia pallida 'Purple Heart' (syn. *Setcreasea pallida* 'Purple Heart', *Setcreasea purpurea*) (Purple heart)

Origin: Eastern Mexico

Decorative interest: This succulent and spreading ground cover is grown for its fleshy and hairy 3-in. leaves that are a regal, violet-purple. Small (¾ in. in diameter), lilac-pink, three-petaled flowers open in the morning and close after noon.

Culture: Full sun for best purple color, normal water, tolerates dry or wet soil.

Height: 6 in. to 18 in.

Propagation: Simple from cuttings. Plants self-seed in the garden.

Horticultural use: Purple heart is indispensable for its rich purple foliage color and ease of culture. Plant it in the foreground of borders and beds, or cascading from con-

tainers with *Strobilanthes dyerianus* and *Cuphea hyssopifolia*. Combine with the reddish-purple *Petunia integrifolia* or bright red flowers like *Pentas lanceolata* and *Ruellia graecizans.*

Overwintering: Take cuttings in the autumn to overwinter as a houseplant on a bright windowsill. Or purchase new plants from garden centers in May. They are sometimes winter-hardy in zone 7 and above.

Tradescantia spathacea (syn. *Rhoeo spathacea, R. discolor*) (Oyster plant, Moses-in-the-boat)

Origin: Southern Mexico, Central America

Decorative interest: This stiff, clumping succulent is architectural. Upright leaves, 8 in. to 15 in. long, green on top and purple on the bottom, whorl around short stems. Small, three-petaled, white flowers emerge from boatlike bracts at the base of the leaf. They're the pearl within the oyster or the baby Moses in his boat. A dwarf cultivar with confused nomenclature exists. It is sometimes listed as *Tradescantia spathacea* 'Minima' or *Rhoeo spathacea* 'Bermudensis'. The cultivar *T. spathacea* 'Vittata' is choice. Golden stripes are on the upper leaf surface, and the lower leaf surface is purple.

Culture: Full sun, normal water, but it survives shade and tolerates moist and dry soils. Warm night temperatures.

Height: 6 in. to 18 in.

Propagation: Seeds, division of rhizomes, or stem cuttings.

Horticultural use: Plant *Tradescantia spathacea* in the foreground of a border or the center of a small container. Grow

Strobilanthes dyerianus, Hemigraphis alternata, heliotrope, or *Lantana montevidensis* nearby. I let red petunias weave through it. Combine *Tradescantia spathacea* 'Vittata' with *Canna* 'Pretoria', *Sanchezia speciosa*, or *Ipomoea batatus* 'Margarita'.

Overwintering: Bring indoors as a house-plant on a warm, bright windowsill. Or purchase new plants in May from specialty garden centers.

Tradescantia zebrina
(syn. *Zebrina pendula*)
(Wandering jew)

Origin: Southern Mexico, Central America

Decorative interest: Rapidly spreading ground cover with beautiful flat leaves, about 2 in. long and 1 in. wide, that are striped with two silver bands. Metallic upper leaf surfaces shimmer; under surfaces are as purple as a Concord grape. Insignificant, three-petaled, triangular, rose-pink flowers,

¾ in., open in the morning. This rather tired-looking indoor houseplant becomes indispensable when planted outdoors.

Culture: Full sun, light shade, normal water, tolerates slightly damp or dry conditions.

Height: 6 in. to 12 in. and often mounding to 18 in. by summer's end.

Propagation: Simple from cuttings.

Horticultural use: Use as a bedding plant in Victorian-style lawn beds around *Tibouchina urvilleana* standards. Position in the foreground of borders, or along the edge of containers, with other bronze-leaved plants like coleus, *Iresine herbstii*, or *Colocasia esculenta* 'Fontanesii'. Combine with the pink-flowered *Justicia carnea*, impatiens, or the violet-blue-flowered *Barleria cristata*.

Overwintering: Root cuttings in October and grow as a houseplant or purchase new plants at any garden center or florist in spring.

COMPOSITAE

Helichrysum petiolare
(Licorice plant)

Origin: South Africa

Decorative interest: This spreading ground cover has rounded, silvery, tomentose leaves, 1 in. to 2 in. in diameter. The leaf color of the popular cultivar *Helichrysum petiolare* 'Limelight' is chartreuse. Where plants are winter-hardy, they produce an everlasting flower like the strawflower, to which it is related. In zone 6 and below *Helichrysum petiolare* is grown as a foliage plant.

Culture: Full sun, normal water, rapid drainage. Keep foliage dry at night.

Height: 6 in. to 1 ft.

Propagation: Stem cuttings.

Horticultural use: Use as an edging plant in containers around *Agave americana* or as a foreground plant in borders. Underplant standards of *Tibouchina urvilleana* with it. Combine *Helichrysum petiolare* with silvery *Plectranthus argentatus* or contrast it with burgundy-leaved *Alternanthera dentata* 'Rubiginosa' and *Hibiscus acetosella* 'Red Shield'. In containers, plant *Ipomoea batatus*

'Blackie' as a cascading companion. Combine *Helichrysum petiolare* 'Limelight' with a pale yellow cultivar of *Lantana camara* and other golden variegated plants like *Phormium tenax* 'Variegata', *Agave americana* 'Marginata', or *Yucca elephantipes* 'Variegata'.

Overwintering: Root stem cuttings in September and grow on a sunny windowsill. Or purchase new plants at garden centers in May.

Pseudogynoxys chenopodioides
(syn. *Senecio confusus*)
(Mexican flamevine)

Origin: Columbia

Decorative interest: This creeping vine is grown for its bright orange, daisylike flowers, up to 2 in. in diameter. Thick, smooth green leaves are about 2 in. long.

Culture: Full sun, normal water.

Height: To 6 ft. on a vine support or to 1 ft. as a spreading ground cover.

Propagation: Stem cuttings in spring or summer.

Horticultural use: Use without support as a ground cover in the foreground of borders combined with bronze foliage, like *Alternanthera dentata* 'Rubiginosa', to intensify the hot color. Or grow it on a vine support with *Thunbergia alata* directly in the ground or in a container with a vine tepee insert. Let it ramble up *Hibiscus acetosella* 'Red Shield'.

Overwintering: Root stem cuttings in September and grow on a sunny windowsill. Or bring plants into a sunny plant room in October (but note that they are prone to scale, aphids, and mealybugs indoors). Or purchase new Florida-grown plants in garden centers in May.

CONVOLVULACEAE

Ipomoea batatus
(Sweet potato)

Origin: Garden hybrid

Decorative interest: I grow *Ipomoea batatus* for its vigorous spreading habit and variable, simple to palmately compound leaves that come in bronze, chartreuse, or variegated. You may grow it for the edible tubers. *Ipomoea batatus* 'Blackie' has been popular for about 10 years. Deeply lobed, palmate, bronze leaves are almost black. Chartreuse-foliaged *Ipomoea batatus* 'Margarita' (photo above), which first became popular in 1997, has leaves that are less deeply lobed.

Culture: Full sun, normal water. *Ipomoea batatus* 'Margarita' is prone to slug damage.

Height: 6 in., trailing to 6 ft.

Propagation: Cuttings or tubers.

Horticultural use: Cascade *Ipomoea batatus* over container rims or use it as a seasonal ground cover in the foreground of a border. Around the rim of a container, intersperse *I. batatus* 'Blackie' with white variegated spider plants for contrast. Use taller chartreuse colors like coleus 'Gold Wizard' behind them. Combine *I. batatus* 'Blackie' with similar inky shades like *Colocasia esculenta* 'Illustris' and coleus 'Inky Fingers'. Blend *Ipomoea batatus* 'Margarita' with coleus 'Gold Wizard', *Alpinia zerumbet* 'Variegata', and *Canna* 'Pretoria'.

Overwintering: Root cuttings in September and grow on a sunny windowsill or dig and dry tubers as you would canna. Or purchase new plants from garden centers in May.

CYCADACEAE

Cycas revoluta
(Sago palm, Dwarf sago)

Origin: Southern Japan

Decorative interest: Grow this rosetted architectural plant for the rich green, feather-palm-like leaves, up to 3 ft. long, that are divided into needle-like leaflets, 3 in. to 6 in. long. This elegant, ancient plant was on the Earth when the dinosaurs roamed; more recently, it was used by the Victorians in subtropical bedding schemes.

Culture: Acclimate to full sun, normal water. Tolerates drier conditions.

Height: 1 ft. to 3 ft.

Propagation: Seed or stem suckers from old plants.

Horticultural use: Architectural plant for specimen or focal use in a border, lawn bed, container, or tub. Use in the center of a formal Victorian-style bedding circle surrounded by rings of the waxed *Begonia semperflorens* or red-leaved caladium.

Overwintering: *Cycas revoluta* is remarkably inexpensive in the houseplant departments of mass-market home stores. New plants can be purchased each spring. However, older plants are special. Over-

winter the sago palm as an easy-to-grow houseplant or keep it alive and semidormant in a cold garage (between 45°F and 55°F) with some light. The related species, *Cycas circinalis*, is a similar but larger plant, 3 ft. to 6 ft. tall, and less common in the houseplant trade. It is from Southeast India and therefore requires warmer overwintering temperatures. Use it as you would *Cycas revoluta* or other true palms.

CYPERACEAE

Cyperus alternifolius
(Umbrella plant)

Origin: Madagascar

Decorative interest: About 12 thin, leaf-like bracts radiate from the top of 3-ft. to 4-ft. triangular stems to resemble the ribs of an umbrella. Leaf coloration is slightly yellowish green. Many stems emerge from the

crown of the plant to form a herbaceous foliar clump.

Culture: Full sun or light shade in water or wet soil. These plants are associated with water gardens but do not require pool conditions. Incorporate water-absorbent planting gels into the planting hole. They are easy to grow and are a naturalized weed throughout the tropical world.

Height: 1 ft. to 4 ft.

Propagation: Divide two-year plants or root the foliage head as you would a stem cutting.

Horticultural use: Use in the middle of borders or in water gardens with *Colocasia esculenta* or *Alocasia macrorrhiza* for textural contrasts. Try a different combination with *Sanchezia speciosa*.

Overwintering: Prune large leaves to the rhizome, divide, and bring divisions indoors to grow as a houseplant in a sunny window with wet soil. Monitor for spider mites in dry indoor environments. Or purchase new plants in May.

EUPHORBIACEAE

Acalypha hispida
(Red hot cat's tail, chenille plant)

Origin: New Guinea, Malaya

Decorative interest: Grow this sparse-stemmed shrub for its dark red, drooping, tassel-like flower spikes, more than 12 in. long, that hang from the leaf axils. Alternate, broadly oval green leaves are 5 in. to 8 in. long and 3 in. wide.

Culture: Full sun or light shade, moist soil. Warm night temperatures. Prune when necessary.

Height: To 6 ft.

Propagation: Stem cuttings in spring and summer.

Horticultural use: Position second-year plants in the middle of the border with bronze-foliage plants like *Alternanthera dentata* 'Rubiginosa' or *Iresine herbstii*. Combine with the dwarf *Canna* 'Crimson Beauty', which has similar flower color but coarser foliage, or the red-flowered *Pentas lanceolata*. The pendulous flower form is interesting when grown in a container. *Acalypha pendula*, a ground-covering species, has similar pendulous flowers that are shorter and more caterpillarlike. It is marketed as a hanging basket plant called "Fuzzy-Wuzzy", but use it as an edging plant in a container design.

Overwintering: Older plants can become large shrubs. Dig and bring indoors to a warm, sunny windowsill or plant room in late September. They prefer warm and humid interior or greenhouse conditions. Monitor for mealybugs. Local or Florida-grown plants can be found in specialty garden centers or nurseries in spring.

Acalypha wilkesiana
(Jacob's coat, copper leaf)

Origin: Pacific Islands

Decorative interest: This shrub is a foliage plant grown for the variable, broad oval, coppery-red or variegated leaves, about 5 in. to 8 in. long and 2 in. to 6 in. wide, that are displayed alternately on the plant. The cultivar 'Macrophylla' (photo above right) has large, reddish variegated leaves, 'Java White' has large, green and white variegated leaves, and 'Marginata' has leaves with a pink margin. All are splendid. *Acalypha godseffiana* 'Heterophylla' is a similar, smaller shrub from New Guinea with small, narrow copper-color leaves with a wavy margin. They are not grown for flowers.

Culture: Full sun for best leaf coloration, moist soil. Warm night temperatures. They can become large shrubs and will benefit from pruning.

Height: 6 in. to 6 ft.

Propagation: Semihard stem cuttings in spring or summer. Can be tricky. Better with bottom heat.

Horticultural use: Position one or three two-year plants in the center of a lawn bed surrounded by rings of *Alternanthera* or coleus or in the middle of a border. Combine *Dracaena marginata* 'Tricolor' and *Justicia brandegeana* around coppery-colored forms.

Overwintering: Treat like *Acalypha hispida*. Small 4-in. pots of *Acalypha godseffiana* 'Heterophylla' are seen in specialty garden centers in spring, and cuttings can mature into 3-ft. plants in a zone 6 growing season.

Breynia nivosa '*Roseapicta*'
(syn. *B. disticha*)
(Snowbush)

Origin: Pacific Islands

Decorative interest: This shrub is grown for its small oval leaves, about 1 in. long, that are mottled red, pink, and white. It is not grown for flowers.

Culture: Full sun for best growth and leaf coloration, normal water, tolerates dappled shade. Warm night temperatures. Prune older plants back to encourage variegation.

Height: 6 in. to 6 ft.

Propagation: Easy from stem cuttings in spring or summer.

Horticultural use: Use in the middle of a border or container with *Pseuderanthemum atropurpureum, Acalypha hispida,* red or pink *Pentas lanceolata,* or *Justicia carnea.*

Overwintering: Older plants can become large shrubs. Dig and bring indoors to a sunny windowsill in late September. They prefer warm and humid interior or greenhouse conditions. Four-inch pots are available in specialty garden centers in May, and cuttings grow to 3 ft. in a single season.

Codiaeum variegatum pictum
(Croton)

Origin: Malaya, Pacific Islands

Decorative use: This shrub is grown for its leathery leaves that range in shape from linear and twisted to oval and oak-leaf-like. Leaf-color combinations seem endless and range from red, bronze, orange, pink, yellow, and gold to green. Hundreds of cultivars exist and are grown as Florida landscape plants, but relatively few are in the houseplant trade. Croton is not grown for flowers.

Culture: Acclimate to full sun for best leaf coloration, though plants tolerate light shade. Normal water, moist, rich soil. Seasonal growth is slow in comparison to *Acalypha* and *Breynia.*

Height: 6 in. to 4 ft.

Propagation: Stem cuttings in spring or air layer.

Horticultural use: Position small, 4-in. pots in the foreground of a border with other bronze and gold-colored foliage or orange-flowered *Lantana camara* and *Cuphea ignea.* Larger specimen plants can go into the middle of the border.

Overwintering: Florida-grown plants are inexpensive and available in garden centers and home stores in all sizes and at all seasons for houseplant use. Acclimate to full sun conditions or leaves will burn and defoliate. By August, new leaves are handsome. Or dig and bring indoors in September to overwinter on a warm, sunny, or bright windowsill. Prune back in spring if leggy.

Euphorbia cotinifolia

Origin: Mexico, South America

Decorative use: This shrubby euphorb is grown for foliage interest. Roundish, coppery-red leaves, 2 in. to 3 in. in diameter, whorl around stems in groups of three.

Culture: Full sun, normal water. Prune to encourage dense foliage growth.

Height: 1 ft. to 6 ft.

Propagation: Stem cuttings in spring and summer.

Horticultural use: Combine with red flowers like *Canna* 'Ambassador', *Pentas lanceolata,* or *Jatropha integerrima.* Train into a standard and underplant with red waxed begonias. As a container plant, pinch for dense growth.

Overwintering: Dig and bring indoors in late September to a warm, sunny windowsill or plant room or greenhouse. Or root stem cuttings in summer and overwinter on a windowsill for next year's display.

Jatropha integerrima
(J. pandurifolia)
(Peregrina)

Origin: Cuba, West Indies

Decorative interest: Grow this plant for its simple, rose-red, five-petaled flowers, about 1 in. in diameter, that are continuously produced. Three-lobed alternate green leaves, about 2 in. long, are always neat. A related species, *Jatropha multifida,* is grown for beautiful, palmately lobed leaves. It is easily propagated from seed and is sold by specialty nurseries. Both are common south Florida landscape plants.

Culture: Full sun or light shade, normal water to slightly dry soil. Warm night temperatures. Prune when necessary.

Height: 6 in. to 4 ft.

Propagation: Stem cuttings in spring.

Horticultural use: Position in the middle of a border with *Acalypha hispida* or red *Pentas lanceolata.* Contrast with burgundy-foliaged plants like *Alternanthera dentata* 'Rubiginosa' or *Pseuderanthemum atropurpureum.*

Overwintering: Root new plants from stem cuttings in summer for next year's display. Older plants can become specimen shrubs. Dig, prune back, and bring indoors to a sunny windowsill or plant room in late September. They prefer warm and humid interior or greenhouse conditions. Or purchase new plants from specialty garden centers in May. Florida-grown standards are occasionally found in the nursery trade.

Manihot esculenta 'Variegata' (Variegated tapioca)

Origin: Brazil

Decorative interest: I grow this stiff-stemmed herbaceous plant for its extraordinarily beautiful, deep palmately lobed, alternate leaves that are creamy-yellow at the center and have carmine-red petioles. Caribbean gardeners grow it for its starchy root.

Culture: Full sun or light shade, normal water to drier soil. Defoliates with pesticide sprays.

Height: 6 in. to 3 ft.

Propagation: Stem cuttings in spring or summer. Use bottom heat.

Horticultural use: Position in the middle of borders with bright yellow *Lantana camara, Allamanda schottii,* or other golden variegated foliage.

Overwintering: Still not common, but this plant is destined soon to become chic. Root new plants from stem cuttings in summer for next year's display. Or dig the tubers, which are the tropical root crop cassava and look like large dahlia tubers. Prepare them like canna.

Ricinus communis (Castor oil plant, castor bean)

Origin: Northeast Africa, Middle East

Decorative interest: This historic plant has been in cultivation for millennia, primarily for castor oil, but in the late 19th century it was grown for "tropical effects." Few plants provide them so grandly and easily. Massive, fan-shaped palmate leaves, 1 ft. to 3 ft. across, each with 5 to 12 deeply cut lobes, are produced on tree-like plants. Lackluster, petal-less female flowers mature into attractive, spiny-skinned poisonous fruits that range in color from gray to scarlet. The cultivar *R. communis* 'Carmencita' (photo below) is one of the best for bronze foliage and bright red fruits; it is dwarf, about 6 ft. to 8 ft.

Culture: Full sun, normal water, tolerates drier soil, requires staking.

Height: 3 ft. to 15 ft.

Propagation: Sow scarified seed into individual pots in late April or early May, or sow directly outdoors in early May.

Horticultural use: Use in the center of Victorian-style lawn beds, with rings of *Canna, Colocasia esculenta,* and coleus around it. Or use in the rear of borders for its bold texture. Because of its poisonous fruits, do not plant where children play.

Overwintering: Treat as an annual and start new seeds each spring.

LABIATAE

Orthosiphon stamineus (Cat's whiskers)

Origin: India

Decorative interest: This shrubby plant is grown for its white or lavender flowers that are produced at the end of stems. Long stamens protrude from flower pairs to resemble the whiskers of a cat. Plants are not in continuous blossom. Glossy green rounded leaves, about 1 in. in diameter, are opposite.

Culture: Full sun or light shade, normal water. Pinch to keep bushy and encourage flowering.

Height: 1 ft. to 3 ft.

Propagation: Easy from stem cuttings at any season. Cuttings taken in April form flowering plants in one growing season.

Horticultural use: Position in the foreground or middle of a border near white variegated or bronze foliage plants. Use as a container plant with various kinds of coleus or *Caladium* 'Candidum'.

Overwintering: Root cuttings in September to overwinter on a warm windowsill or greenhouse. Or purchase new plants from garden centers in May.

Plectranthus argentatus (Silver-leafed plectranthus)

Origin: Australia

Decorative interest: Grow this shrubby plant for its silvery, hairy leaves, 2 in. to 4 in. long, that are opposite each other. Delicate spikes of insignificant whitish flowers top the stems.

Culture: Full sun or light shade, normal water.

Height: 1 ft. to 3 ft. Prune if it becomes too large.

Propagation: Easy from cuttings at any season. Cuttings taken in April form full-size plants in one growing season.

Horticultural use: Position in the foreground of borders in front of *Tibouchina urvilleana* or contrast with *Alternanthera dentata* 'Rubiginosa', *Hibiscus acetosella* 'Red Shield', or *Ipomoea batatas* 'Blackie'.

Artemisia 'Powis Castle' is similar in leaf color but has a fine-filigreed foliage. Use it to contrast textures.

Overwintering: Root cuttings in September to overwinter on a warm windowsill or greenhouse. Or purchase new plants from garden centers in May.

Plectranthus forsteri 'Marginatus' (Variegated plectranthus)

Origin: New Caledonia

Decorative interest: This shrubby foliage plant is grown for its velvety, broad oval leaves with strong, 2½-in.- to 4-in.-long scalloped white margins that are produced opposite each other along the stem. *Plectranthus madagascariensis* 'Variegated Mintleaf' is a similar trailing form with smaller leaves.

Culture: Full sun or light shade, normal water. Can be trained into a standard. fast grower.

Height: 1 ft. to 4 ft.

Propagation: Easy from cuttings. Cuttings taken in April form full-size plants in one growing season.

Horticultural use: Position in the foreground of borders to contrast with *Alternanthera dentata* 'Rubiginosa', *Hibiscus acetosella* 'Red Shield', and *Tradescantia pallida* 'Purple Heart'. Grow as a standard in the center of a container with cascades of *Ipomoea batatus* 'Blackie'.

Overwintering: Root cuttings in September to overwinter on a warm windowsill or greenhouse. Or purchase new plants from garden centers in May.

LILIACEAE

Asparagus densiflorus (Asparagus fern)

Origin: South Africa

Decorative interest: Two cultivars are popular foliage plants. *Asparagus densiflorus* 'Myersii' (photo above), the foxtail fern, is grown for its somewhat architectural, erect foxtail-shaped stems, 15 in. long and 2½ in. wide. *Asparagus densiflorus* 'Sprengeri' (syn. *A. sprengeri*), the sprenger fern, is grown for its loose and drooping fernlike stems, up to 3 ft. long, with ½-in. to 1-in. needle-like leaves.

Culture: Full sun, normal water. Benefits from liquid fertilization.

Height: 1 ft. to 3 ft.

Propagation: Division of clumps or seed.

Horticultural use: Position in the foreground of borders or in containers. Pots of *Asparagus densiflorus* 'Myersii' can be placed above ground in the foreground or middle of the border, without planting. Nearby plants grow quickly to hide the container, and the *Asparagus densiflorus* 'Myersii' foliage appears taller than it actually is. It is a simple way to rejuvenate houseplants during the summer. Place the pot on top of newspaper to prevent roots from entering the soil through the drainage hole. Or grow in clay pots to position as architectural plants. Use *Asparagus densiflorus* 'Sprengeri' to cascade over the rim of a large container with *Chlorophytum comosum* 'Vittatum' and *Cordyline indivisa* as the center spike for a fine texture effect.

Overwintering: Asparagus ferns always drop their needle-like leaves and are messy houseplants. Bring them indoors in late September and place them on a sunny windowsill for best growth. Or to achieve large, specimen plants, dig, pot, and bring plants into a cool but frost-free garage or basement, preferably with some light, about November 1. Prune old stems in spring and liquid fertilize. Or purchase new plants from garden centers in spring to use as container plants.

Chlorophytum comosum 'Vittatum' (Spider plant)

Origin: South Africa

Decorative interest: This foliage plant forms a herbaceous rosette of arching 1-ft.-long linear leaves that are medium green with a central white or cream stripe. Plantlets form at the end of weak stems and weigh them down. Small, six-petaled white flowers, 1 in. in diameter, are insignificant.

Culture: Light shade or acclimate to full sun. Leaves initially sunburn, but plants soon flourish in bright sunlight. Normal water. Tolerates cool night temperatures.

Height: 6 in. to 18 in.

Propagation: Remove and pot up stem plantlets.

Horticultural use: Use as an edging plant around Victorian-style lawn beds with *Canna* or *Colocasia esculenta* inside. Position in the foreground of borders near other white variegated plants like *Plectranthus forsteri* 'Marginatus' or contrast with burgundy-foliaged plants like *Alternanthera dentata* 'Rubiginosa' and coleus. Place three spider plants along the edge of a container to hang downward or grow them in a hanging basket.

Overwintering: Pot up plantlets in September to use as houseplants and for propagation stock. Easy to grow in most indoor environments. Or purchase in the houseplant section of garden centers in May.

Gloriosa superba
(Climbing lily)

Origin: Tropical Africa

Decorative interest: This is a tuberous lily-like plant that grows as a weak-stemmed vine. Tendrils at the leaf tip cling to other plants or vine supports. Six deep orange and yellow or chartreuse petals, near 3 in. long, are angled backward like a shooting star; 12 to 18 form on the stem and last almost one month.

Culture: Carefully plant the brittle tubers in good soil so that the growing tip is just below the soil surface. Plant in full sun, provide normal water.

Height: 3 ft. to 5 ft.

Propagation: Division of tubers after the vine withers away.

Horticultural use: Grow on a vine support in the foreground or middle of a border. Or let it ramble through the stems of other shrubs, like *Tecomaria capensis* or *Pseuderanthemum atropurpureum*. Grow as a container specimen on a vine tepee.

Overwintering: Dig tubers after foliage withers away and store in dry sawdust or peat moss. Bring container specimens into a cool but frost-free garage or basement. Or purchase new tubers from bulb catalogs in spring.

LYTHRACEAE

Cuphea hyssopifolia
(Elfin herb, false heather)

Origin: Mexico, Guatemala

Decorative interest: This short, shrubby ground cover is grown for small, six-petaled flowers, up to ½ in. across, in shades of purple, pink, or white. Green leaves are about ¾ in. long.

Culture: Full sun, normal water.

Height: 6 in. to 18 in.

Propagation: Easy from stem cuttings at any time.

Horticultural use: Position in the foreground of a border or in a container with *Strobilanthes dyerianus*, *Tradescantia pallida* 'Purple Heart', and *Lantana montevidensis*.

Overwintering: Root cuttings in September to overwinter as a houseplant on a sunny windowsill. Or purchase new plants in May.

Cuphea ignea
(syn. *C. platycentra*)
(Cigar flower, firecracker plant)

Origin: Mexico, Jamaica

Decorative use: This small, shrubby plant is grown for the 1-in. orange-red, tubular flowers that are constantly produced. Two-inch-long leaves develop a reddish edge in full sunshine. The cultivar *Cuphea ignea* 'David Verity' (photo above) is taller, up to 4 ft., and more erect in habit. Flowers are more orange than red.

Culture: Full sun, normal water. Tolerates drier conditions.

Height: 1 ft. to 4 ft.

Propagation: Easy from cuttings at any time.

Horticultural use: *Cuphea ignea* is a historic plant that was grown in Victorian lawn beds. To achieve a similar bedding display, space plants about 9 in. apart and pinch stem tips. Plants then branch and become bushy. Ring them around *Salvia splendens* and *Canna* 'The President' for a fiery display. Use *Cuphea ignea* 'David Verity' in the foreground or middle of a hot-colored border with *Lantana camara* 'Radiation'. Burgundy foliage, like *Hibiscus acetosella* 'Red Shield', intensifies the hot color.

Overwintering: Root cuttings in September to overwinter as houseplants on a sunny window. Use these as stock plants and take additional cuttings in early April to increase your plant numbers.

MALVACEAE

Abutilon pictum 'Thompsonii' (syn. *A. striatum*) (Variegated flowering maple)

Origin: Brazil

Decorative interest: This weak-stemmed shrub or small tree is grown mostly for its yellow mottled leaves, 3 in. to 6 in. long, with three to five lobes, that resemble those of a maple. Five-petaled, salmon-pink flowers dangle downward.

Culture: Full sun, normal water, cooler temperatures. Prune to encourage dense foliage growth.

Height: To 5 ft.

Propagation: Stem cuttings in spring and summer.

Horticultural use: Use in Victorian-style lawn beds around yellow-flowered canna or *Canna* 'Pretoria'. Position them in the middle of borders with other golden variegated plants or grow in containers with *Ipomoea batatus* 'Margarita'. Flower color blends with the fruit color of *Duranta erecta*. Train as a standard or pyramid.

Overwintering: Root cuttings in September to overwinter on a sunny windowsill or greenhouse. Plants are prone to whitefly indoors. Or purchase new plants in May.

Hibiscus acetosella 'Red Shield' (syn. *H. eetveldeanus*) (Maroon-leaved hibiscus)

Origin: East and Central Africa

Decorative interest: This shrubby, herbaceous plant is grown for its brilliant maroon, five-lobed leaves. In late autumn, dusty-maroon-colored flowers about 1½ in. in diameter appear from the leaf axils. Two distinct leaf forms are called 'Red Shield' in the nursery trade.

Culture: Full sun, normal water. Stake and pinch to keep neat and full.

Height: To 5 ft.

Propagation: Easy from stem cuttings when not in flower.

Horticultural use: Position in the middle of a border near red flowers like *Hibiscus rosa-sinensis*. Contrast the maroon foliage with white or golden variegated plants, such as *Ananas comosus* 'Variegatus' or silver foliage like *Plectranthus argentatus*. Staked and sheared plants can form a seasonal hedge.

Overwintering: Root cuttings in September to overwinter on a sunny windowsill or greenhouse. Or purchase new plants in May.

Hibiscus rosa-sinensis (Hawaiian hibiscus)

Origin: Tropical Asia

Decorative interest: Large, branching shrub, up to and over 5 ft. tall, is grown for its large (about 6 in. in diameter), five-petaled flowers that are continually produced. Each individual flower lasts only one day. Red is the commonest color, but hybrids are in every shade but blue. The cultivar *Hibiscus rosa-sinensis* 'Cooperi' is grown for beautiful variegated leaves that shimmer in tones of green, white, red, and pink. Smaller, clear red flowers are pendulous on the end of stems.

Culture: Full sun, normal water. Prune when leggy.

Height: 2 ft. to 4 ft., or standard, 3 ft. to 5 ft.

Propagation: Stem cuttings in spring or summer.

Horticultural use: Use as a container plant or grow specimens in tubs. Standards are common. Position in foreground, middle, or rear of the border depending on the size of the plant. Combine with other appropriate, analagous flower colors. Combine *Hibiscus rosa-sinensis* 'Cooperi' with *Breynia nivosa*, white variegated, and bronze-foliaged plants.

Overwintering: Dig, pot, and bring plants into a warm (tolerates cool, 55°F.) and sunny greenhouse or plant room in early October. Plants are prone to whitefly. Prune back in early spring. Or purchase new Florida-grown plants inexpensively at garden centers in May.

MARANTACEAE

Maranta leuconeura (Prayer plant)

Origin: Brazil

Decorative interest: *Maranta* is a common indoor foliage plant grown for its glaucous oval leaves, about 6 in. long and 2 in. wide, that display pronounced pale veins with blackish markings between them. The under surface is purplish. Flowers are insignificant. Outdoors it takes on a spreading habit and acts as a seasonal ground cover.

Culture: Light shade, normal water, warm temperatures. Plants acclimate to higher light levels and survive cooler temperatures.

Height: 6 in. to 1 ft.

Propagation: Division of older clumps or stem cuttings.

Horticultural use: I use *Maranta leuconeura* as a herbaceous ground cover beneath *Colocasia esculenta* 'Fontanesii'. Their foliage colors harmonize well. Use it as a foreground planting in shady borders.

Overwintering: Dig, pot, and bring indoors in late September as an easy to grow houseplant in medium light. Or purchase new plants in the houseplant section of garden centers in May.

MELASTOMATACEAE

Tibouchina urvilleana
(syn. *T. semidecandra*)
(Glory bush)

Origin: Brazil

Decorative interest: This tree-like shrub is grown for the regal purple flowers that form in clusters at the end of branches. Each lasts only a day, then drops to let other buds open. They are produced after day lengths begin to shorten. Paired oval leaves, about 4 in. long, are hairy and soft as velvet. Their coloration is slightly glaucous green.

Culture: Full sun, normal water. Prune back weak branches and shape plant when planting outdoors. Can be trained into a standard. Propagate cuttings for next year's display.

Height: 3 ft. to 6 ft.

Propagation: Stem cuttings in spring or summer.

Horticultural use: Position in the middle to rear of borders in combination with other glaucous green and silver foliage like *Colocasia esculenta* 'Fontanesii' and *Plectranthus argentatus*. The purple flowers of *Salvia leucantha* occur in October when *Tibouchina* is in peak bloom. Place it in front of the glory bush to hide the exposed stems. Use standards in the center of beds or as container plants.

Overwintering: To achieve large standards, dig, pot, and bring plants into a cool, sunny plant room in early November. Plants that aren't too large can become houseplants on a sunny windowsill. Root cuttings in spring or summer to become next year's display plants. Or purchase new plants from nurseries and garden centers in May.

MORACEAE

Ficus elastica
(Rubber plant)

Origin: Southeast Asia

Decorative interest: *Ficus elastica*, like most other species in the genus *Ficus*, is grown for its attractive shiny foliage. Large leaves, up to 15 in. long, give the exotic garden a distinct tropical look. Leaf size, shape,

shade, and variegation are variable and depend on the cultivar chosen. *Ficus elastica* 'Robusta Variegata' (photo below) has beautiful, broad-oval leaves that are marked like marble in gray, white, and pink.

Culture: Variegated-leaf cultivars require higher light levels, with some sunshine, than all-green cultivars. Normal water.

Height: Variable to 8 ft. In the tropics, the rubber plant is a tree that grows 200 ft. tall. Not so in temperate gardens, where heights are easier to control.

Propagation: Air layer.

Horticultural use: Position older, larger specimens in the rear of borders, and younger, smaller specimens in the middle or even foreground. Place houseplants on top of the soil surface, then hide the pot by planting coleus in its foreground. Contrast the coarse foliage of *Ficus elastica* with the stiff foliage of architectural plants like *Dracaena marginata* 'Tricolor' or *Pandanus veitchii*.

Overwintering: Dig, pot, and bring plants indoors in early October as an easy-to-grow houseplant. Or purchase new plants inexpensively from garden centers and home stores in May.

MUSACEAE

Ensete ventricosum 'Maurelii'
(syn. *Musa ensete*)
(Red Abyssinian banana)

Origin: Africa

Decorative interest: This handsome, non-suckering banana is grown for its compact rosette of large and broad, 10-ft.-long and

4-ft.-wide, paddle-shaped leaves that are tinged red and whorl around a single trunk. *Ensete ventricosum* 'Maurelii' is more architectural in form than bananas of the genus *Musa*. Bananas are herbaceous tree-like plants that die after they flower and fruit, which occurs on some second-year plants in zone 6 gardens.

Culture: Full sun for best color, rich moist soil, warm humid conditions. Protect from strong wind. Plants grow fast with proper soil, water, fertilizer, and temperature.

Height: To 10 ft.

Propagation: Seed.

Horticultural use: Any and all banana varieties are essential components of the exotic garden. Their form and texture spell exoticism, now as much as in the 19th century. Plant them directly into the soil, keep them in their pot, or grow them as a specimen tub. Simple tubs of banana are elegant additions to a poolside patio. The reddish foliage color of *Ensete ventricosum* 'Maurelii' intensifies hot flower colors and variegated foliage. Position plants in the middle or rear of borders or in the center of a Victorian-style lawn bed. Use with *Canna* 'Ambassador', *Colocasia esculenta*, or *Ricinus communis* 'Carmencita' and edge with red caladium or waxed begonias.

Overwintering: Dig, pot, and bring small, manageable plants into a warm or cool, sunny greenhouse or plant room in late October. They will survive in a cool but frost-free garage. Sow seed in the summer to plant outdoors next May. Or purchase new plants from garden centers in May or from southern mail-order nurseries to arrive at planting time.

Musa acuminata (syn. *M. cavendishii*) (Banana)

Origin: Southeast Asia

Decorative interest: These suckering bananas are grown for their handsome, large leaves that whorl from the top of a stately tree-like trunk. Some are blotched burgundy, rare ones are variegated with white stripes. The dwarf form, *Musa acuminata* 'Dwarf Cavendish', when planted in fertile soil grows about 6 ft. to 9 ft. tall, and in its second year may produce flowers and fruits. It is the most widespread banana clone in existence. The leaves of a related species (perhaps a form of *M. acuminata*) called *Musa sumatrana*, the bloodleaf banana, are near 8 ft., blotched wine-red above, and stained red beneath. Plants top 14 ft. in height. Numerous cultivars of *M. acuminata* are grown commercially throughout the tropical world for fruit. Ornamental bananas, *M. ornata* and *M. velutina*, are grown for attractively colored (red and pink) flowers and fruit.

Culture: Full sun, rich moist soil, warm humid conditions. Protect from strong wind; however, leaves tear naturally along their veins, which is part of the banana appeal. Plants grow fast with proper soil, water, fertilizer, and temperatures. *Musa acuminata* 'Dwarf Cavendish' is adapted to growth in cool climates better than other tropical bananas. Dwarf plants, about 6 ft. tall, are less susceptible to wind damage than taller varieties and are excellent for container culture.

Height: To 15 ft.

Propagation: Offshoots, division of corm, or seed.

Horticultural use: Same as *Ensete ventricosum* 'Maurelii'. Combine with palms for a very tropical garden.

Overwintering: Dig, pot, and bring small, manageable plants or offshoots from parent plants into a sunny greenhouse or plant room in late October. Prune away tattered leaves. Or purchase new plants from garden centers in May or from southern mail-order nurseries to arrive at planting time.

NYCTAGINACEAE

Bougainvillea glabra (Paper flower)

Origin: Brazil

Decorative interest: The generic name, "bougainvillea," is probably more common than the common name "paper flower." Caribbeans nickname them "bougs." Whatever you call these weak-stemmed, viny shrubs that are armed with spines, they are extraordinarily showy. Hundreds of hybrids and cultivars exist, each with a different size, habit, floral color, or leaf variegation. The fluorescent pink, orange, gold, red, and purple flowers that cluster at the end of branches are really clusters of three papery bracts (hence paper flower) that surround small white flowers.

Culture: Full sun, normal water to slightly dry conditions. Do not plant directly into the ground. Keep in clay pots and allow them to dry between watering. This keeps plants flowering. Avoid high-nitrogen fertilizers, which encourage lush foliage at the expense of flowers. Prune to keep under control. Tolerates cold temperatures.

Height: 2 ft. to 8 ft.

Propagation: Stem cuttings in summer.

Horticultural use: Bougainvillea evokes images of hillside Mediterranean villages where enormous plants enshroud homes with red-tiled roofs. Combine them with other plants that evoke similar Mediterranean images like date palms, jasmine, and *Aloe vera.* Grow them as a specimen plant on a vine support in a terra-cotta container and use them on a poolside patio.

Overwintering: Bring pots into a cool, sunny greenhouse or plant room (but note that plants are prone to whitefly indoors and leaves tend to drop). Prune away tangled growth. Purchase new plants in May (they're common in garden centers).

PALMAE

Chamaerops humilis
(Mediterranean fan palm)

Origin: Mediterranean

Decorative interest: Palms are grown for unique textural effects. The Mediterranean fan palm is a neat, shrubby, multistemmed palm with stiff fan-shaped, gray-green fronds about 2 ft. across.

Culture: Light shade or acclimate to full sun, normal water.

Height: 3 ft. to 8 ft.

Propagation: Seed.

Horticultural use: Use palms outdoors for distinct tropical effects. The gray-green foliage color of *Chamaerops humilis* harmo-

nizes with the foliage of *Tibouchina urvilleana, Plectranthus argentatus, Lantana camara,* or *Aloe vera.* Position in the middle or rear of borders, or grow as a container or tub specimen.

Overwintering: Bring indoors as a houseplant in mid-October. Allow plant to go slightly dormant (cooler temperatures, 55°F to 60°F, reduced water and fertilizer) during the winter months. Acclimate to full sun before planting outdoors next May.

Livistona chinensis
(Chinese fan palm)

Origin: Southern Japan, southern Taiwan

Decorative interest: Grow these fan palms for their 2-ft.-wide and 2-ft.-long glossy green fronds that are deeply cut into many drooping segments. Frond bases appear pleated. In the wild, these palms develop into tall trees, but in northern homes and gardens they remain short single- or multitrunk plants.

Culture: Light shade or acclimate to full sun, normal water.

Height: 2 ft. to 8 ft.

Propagation: Seed.

Horticultural use: *Livistona chinensis* is a common palm species that was popular in Victorian times. Plant it in the center of Victorian-style lawn circles or in the center of a Victorian cast-iron vase. Position the vase in the center of a lawn bed with common Victorian bedding plants around it. Pots of *Livistona chinensis* are effective porch decorations and can grow well without sun. Or use them as architectural plants in the foreground or middle of borders.

Overwintering: Bring plants indoors in early October as an easy-to-grow houseplant in bright light and normal to cool room temperatures. Or purchase new plants next May.

Ravenea rivularis
(Majesty palm)

Origin: Uncertain

Decorative interest: This is a feather palm grown for long delicate fronds that resemble those of the more common areca palm (but aren't golden). The fronds become animated in the garden with every breeze. Plants are single-trunked trees.

Culture: Light shade or acclimate to full sun, normal water.

Height: 3 ft. to 8 ft.

Propagation: Seed.

Horticultural use: Plant in the center of Victorian-style lawn circles with ribbons of canna, caladium, coleus, or other Victorian bedding plants around it. Like *Livistona, Ravenea* are effective plants for porch containers. Or use them as architectural plants in the foreground or middle of borders. Contrast with coarse-foliaged plants, like *Ficus elastica.*

Overwintering: Bring indoors in early October as an easy-to-grow houseplant in bright light and normal room temperatures. Prune old tattered fronds at their base. Or purchase new plants next May; they have become widely available and are inexpensive in most home stores.

PANDANACEAE

Pandanus sp.
(Screw pine)

Origin: Madagascar, tropical Asia

Decorative interest: *Pandanus* is a genus of architectural foliar plants grown for long, linear, leathery leaves that spiral around the stem like threads on a screw. Their nomenclature is confused. Most species have green leaves with a serrated edge, which can cut skin like a knife. *Pandanus baptistii* 'Aurea', the Timor screw pine, is the exception and jewel of the group. Leaves, free of spines, have a beautiful gold stripe down their center. The dark green, spiny leaves of *Pandanus veitchii* (photo below) have a narrow white stripe lengthwise near their edge. However, leaves sometimes revert to all green. *Pandanus sanderi* is similar in leaf form but is golden in color. All are large woody shrubs in the tropics, but in northern greenhouses and gardens their habit more closely resembles that of a pineapple. *Pandanus utilis*, the true screw pine from Madagascar, is a large single-trunked tree.

Culture: Full sun, moist soil, warm night temperatures.

Height: 1 ft. to 6 ft.

Propagation: Remove and pot suckers.

Horticultural use: Use *Pandanus* as you would use other architectural plants in containers, beds, or borders. Position *Pandanus baptistii* 'Aurea' in the middle of borders with other golden variegated plants like *Sanchezia speciosa* or near *Allamanda cathartica*.

Overwintering: *Pandanus veitchii* is the most common species in the trade and is often found in garden centers in May. *Pandanus baptistii* 'Aurea' will require a greater search. Once found, overwinter it as a special houseplant on a warm sunny windowsill or in a plant room or greenhouse with moist soil and high humidity.

PASSIFLORACEAE

Passiflora sp.
(Passion flower vine)

Origin: Tropical America

Decorative interest: *Passiflora* is a large genus of vigorous vines that attach themselves to any support by spiraling tendrils. Green leaves, about 4 in. across, are deeply palmately lobed. *Passiflora caerulea*, the blue passion flower from Brazil and Argentina, is grown for its dramatic 3-in.-wide, cup-shaped flowers. A ring of five white sepals and five white petals, similar in appearance, encircle a wheel of stamens that are bluish purple. *Passiflora coccinea* (photo above), the red passion flower from the Guianas, Southern Venezuela, Peru, Bolivia, and Brazil, is grown for its flower of similar form (but different, scarlet red color).

Culture: Full sun, normal water. Prune when needed.

Height: Over 8 ft. in a growing season.

Propagation: Stem cuttings in summer.

Horticultural use: Plant passion flower vines on a vine support of some kind, like a pergola. In containers, grow them up a vine tepee. Intertwine the blue trumpet vine, *Thunbergia grandiflora*, with *Passiflora caerulea*, and the red morning glory, *Ipomoea coccinea*, with *Passiflora coccinea*.

Overwintering: Bring pots of *Passiflora caerulea* indoors in early October as a houseplant in a sunny window or plant room. Ideal interior winter temperature is a cool 50°F. It may be winter-hardy in zone 7 and above. *Passiflora coccinea* requires warmer and more humid interior winter conditions. Root cuttings in summer and overwinter as a houseplant on a sunny windowsill to plant outdoors the following May. Or purchase Florida-grown plants in garden centers in May.

PIPERACEAE

Peperomia magnoliifolia 'Jellie'
(Jellie peperomia)

Origin: West Indies, northern South America

Decorative interest: This is a robust, semi-succulent foliage plant with weak stems that crawl horizontally, forming a ground cover. In Barbados, *Peperomia magnoliifolia* creeps on top of coralstone boulders, covering them. Thick, glossy green leaves, 4 in. to 6 in., resemble a small leaf of the southern magnolia *(Magnolia grandifolia)* but are marbled cream and pink in the cultivar *Peperomia magnoliifolia* 'Jellie'.

Culture: Light shade, acclimate to sun, normal water. Allow to dry slightly between watering.

Height: 6 in. to 1 ft.

Propagation: Easy from cuttings.

Horticultural use: Use this plant in the foreground of semishady borders with *Aphelandra squarrosa* or in containers with *Cordyline fruticosa*. I grow it in the shade beneath a garden bench.

Overwintering: Dig, pot, and bring *Peperomia magnoliifolia* 'Jellie' indoors in late September or root cuttings in summer to overwinter as an easy-to-grow houseplant. Or purchase new plants from the houseplant section of garden centers in May.

PLUMBAGINACEAE

Plumbago auriculata (syn. *P. capensis*) (Cape leadwort)

Origin: South Africa

Decorative interest: *Plumbago auriculata* is a weak-stemmed shrub prized for its sky-blue, five-petaled flowers, about 1 in. in diameter, that are frequently borne in clusters at the end of stems. Darker blue and white-flowered forms exist.

Culture: Full sun, normal water, tolerates cool temperatures. Prune when needed.

Height: 2 ft. to 6 ft.

Propagation: Stem cuttings in spring or summer.

Horticultural use: Compose *Plumbago auriculata* into a terra-cotta container garden with *Chamaerops humilis*, *Bougainvillea*, *Plectranthus australis*, and *Tradescantia pallida* 'Purple Heart'. *Plumbago* is vinelike and can be trained to grow up a wall or vine support. Place a vine tepee inside the container and train *Plumbago* into a pyramidal topiary. Specimen tubs can be positioned strategically into formal designs. Outside the exotic garden they combine well with Mediterranean herbs like rosemary and sage. Plants respond well to pruning and can be trimmed into globular or hedge forms. *Plumbago* blooms about 28 days after pruning. Old specimens can be cut to the ground in spring.

Overwintering: Bring specimen tubs into a cool and sunny greenhouse, plant room, or frost-free garage. Root cuttings in summer, overwinter on a cool, sunny windowsill, then use in containers the following season. However, two-year-old plants are best. Purchase new California- or Oregon-grown plants from garden centers in spring. Plants are winter-hardy in zone 8 and above.

POLYGONACEAE

Antigonon leptopus (Coral vine, corallita, confederate vine)

Origin: Mexico

Decorative interest: Grow this vigorous viny species for its bubble-gum-pink flowers, composed of five petal-like sepals, that are prolifically produced in spike-like sprays of 6 to 20 blooms. They form at the end of stems and in leaf axils. A tendril at the end of each spray adheres the vine to its support. Leaves are alternate, 3 in. to 5 in. long, heart-shaped, and crinkled.

Culture: Full sun, normal water, tolerates drier conditions, cool temperatures, and low humidity. Prune as needed.

Height: To 8 ft.; older specimens grow taller, depending on culture.

Propagation: Stem cuttings in summer.

Horticultural use: Grow as a container specimen and train on a vine tepee insert. Or position the container at the base of a trellis or pergola and attach the stems to it. Plants grown directly in rich soil remain vegetative. Do not overfertilize—the finest flowers are produced in infertile soil.

Overwintering: Cut vines to their base after the top growth is damaged by low temperatures and bring containers into a cool (45°F to 55°F) garage or basement with minimum light. Withhold water. In spring, increase light and water and position containers outdoors. Growth resumes from tuberous roots. Provide a liquid-fertilizer boost to encourage a good foliage start.

PUNICACEAE

Punica granatum (Pomegranate)

Origin: Eastern Mediterranean to Himalayas

Decorative interest: Pomegranates are shrubby plants that have been cultivated since ancient times for their refreshing fruit. Brilliant bell-shaped blossoms composed of curious, 1-in.-long, crinkled orange-red petals dangle at the end of stems and give rise to the coveted crimson, juicy fruit. Each fruit is protected with a leathery skin that ripens brownish yellow or purplish red and is crowned by a thick calyx. Glossy, lance-shaped leaves, about 3 in. long, are bright green. A dwarf form, *Punica granatum* 'Nana', fruits freely, and a white-fruited form also exists.

Culture: Full sun, normal water. Renewal-prune older, twiggy plants by cutting old stems to the ground in spring.

Height: 3 ft. to 6 ft.

Propagation: Hardwood cuttings or side-shoot cuttings with a heel attached.

Horticultural use: Create a terra-cotta orchard with specimen pots of citrus, date palms, and figs. Or strategically position

pomegranate pots into the design of a formal herb or knot garden to exoticize it. The poisonous oleander is a traditional companion.

Overwintering: Let plants harden for winter outdoors until they receive a light frost, then bring them into a cool garage, where they will survive the winter at temperatures just above freezing. They may drop their leaves. *Punica granatum* 'Nana' can be brought indoors to a cool, sunny windowsill or plant room.

RUBIACEAE

Ixora coccinea (Jungle geranium)

Origin: India, Sri Lanka

Decorative interest: Handsome and neat *Ixora* shrubs are always in flower. Small, ½-in., four-petaled blossoms, in shades of pink, salmon, yellow, orange, or red, cluster together to form flat-topped flower heads, 2 in. to 4 in. in diameter. Glossy, oval, dark green leaves are in pairs. Shrubs are slow growing. Dwarf forms exist.

Culture: Sun, normal water, high humidity, warm night temperatures.

Height: 6 in. to 3 ft.

Propagation: Stem cuttings in spring.

Horticultural use: Position in the foreground of borders. Combine clear pink cultivars with *Iresine herbstii* and *Justicia carnea*. Contrast salmon and tangerine shades with copper-colored forms of *Acalypha wilkesiana* or *Alternanthera ficoidea*.

Overwintering: As a houseplant, *Ixora* requires sun, warm temperatures, and high humidity. If you give it good interior conditions, it will reward you with flowers all winter long. Dig, pot, and bring plants indoors to a sunny windowsill, plant room, or greenhouse in mid-September. Or purchase new Florida-grown plants from garden centers in May.

Pentas lanceolata (Egyptian star cluster)

Origin: Eastern Africa

Decorative interest: This soft-wooded, bushy shrub is grown for the 3-in. clusters of small (about ½-in.), five-petaled, red, pink, lavender, or white flowers. Blossoms appear most of the summer but increase in quantity when day lengths start to shorten. Green, lance-shaped leaves are 3 in. to 4 in. long, hairy, and in pairs.

Culture: Full sun, normal water.

Height: 1 ft. to 4 ft.

Propagation: Easy from cuttings

Horticultural use: Position red *Pentas* in the foreground or middle of borders with *Pseuderanthemum atropurpureum, Ruellia graecizans,* and *Acalypha hispida*. New dwarf pink, lavender, and white cultivars are good bedding plants.

Overwintering: Root cuttings in September to overwinter as a houseplant on a sunny windowsill or in a greenhouse. Plants are prone to whiteflies. Or purchase new plants at garden centers in May.

RUTACEAE

X*Citrofortunella microcarpa* (Calamondin orange)

Origin: Garden hybrid

Decorative interest: The calamondin is just one of several kinds of citrus trees that can be summered outdoors in a temperate garden. Leathery and lustrous leaves of all citrus species are dark and handsome, and five-petaled white flowers, about 1 in. in diameter, are deliciously fragrant. But the form and fruit of the calamondin is especially attractive. Small, spherical fruits, 1 in. to 1½ in., ripen bright orange in the autumn and remain ornamental during the winter months as an interior plant. Plants are easily grown as small shrubs but are more decorative when grown as standards. Trunks are straighter than most other citrus varieties, and the bark is smooth and blackish gray.

Culture: Full sun, normal water, prune as needed.

Height: 1 ft. to 6 ft.

Propagation: Cultivars are usually budded onto rootstock. Stem cuttings in spring.

Horticultural use: Citrus are best in a terra-cotta pot as part of the container garden. They associate well with other Mediterranean plants, like pomegranate, oleander, and *Aloe vera*. Alternate pots of citrus standards with oleander down the length of a swimming-pool patio. Use them in pivotal architectural positions to exoticize the design of a formal garden, like a herb or rose garden.

Overwintering: Florida- and California-grown citrus standards are often sold in

garden centers as patio plants in May. Six inch calamondin pots are always available. Bring plants indoors to a cool, sunny plant room or greenhouse with high humidity in October. Cool autumn night temperatures (below 50°F) help to color maturing fruit. Reduce water and encourage winter dormancy but don't allow pots to dry completely.

Murraya paniculata
(syn. *M. exotica)*
(Orange jessamine,
orange jasmine)

Origin: India, China, Southeast Asia

Decorative interest: Grow this plant for the white, citruslike flowers that are more fragrant than citrus. Small red fruits ripen afterwards. Pinnately compound leaves are dark green and glossy. Shrubby *Murraya paniculata* plants are easily trained into hedges, topiary, small trees, or standards.

Culture: Full sun, normal water, prune as needed.

Height: 2 ft. to 8 ft.

Propagation: Stem cuttings in spring.

Horticultural use: Use this easy-to-grow plant in a container like citrus.

Overwintering: Bring pots of *Murraya paniculata* indoors to a warm, sunny, and humid windowsill, plant room, or greenhouse in late September. Or purchase new Florida-grown plants in garden centers in May for outdoor use.

SCROPHULARIACEAE

Russelia equisetiformis
(Coral plant)

Origin: Mexico

Decorative interest: This shrub is grown for its unique, horsetail-like habit. Weak stems are pendulous, green, and often leafless. Coral-red tubular flowers, about 1 in. in length, are produced in large clusters.

Culture: Full sun, moist soil. Prune old specimens hard to rejuvenate.

Height: 1 ft. to 3 ft.

Propagation: Division or cuttings.

Horticultural use: *Russelia*'s pendulous habit makes it desirable for hanging baskets and containers. Let it cascade from a large container with the architectural *Cordyline indivisa* or *Phormium tenax* 'Purpureum' in its center. Or use in the foreground of a border as a ground cover near the coppery-

colored *Acalypha wilkesiana* or *Acalypha godseffiana* 'Heterophylla'.

Overwintering: Bring plants indoors as hanging baskets in sunny windows, plant rooms, or greenhouses in early October. Or cut back and place on a warm, sunny windowsill. Keep slightly dry until spring, then, as days get long and sunny, water to encourage growth. Propagate from cuttings in summer and overwinter on a sunny windowsill for next year's garden.

SOLANACEAE

Brugmansia x *candida*
(syn. *Datura* x *candida)*
(Angel's trumpet)

Origin: Garden hybrid

Decorative interest: This soft-wooded, tree-like shrub is a showstopper. Elliptic leaves, about 6 in. to 8 in. long, are large, coarse, and very tropical-looking. But *Brugmansia* is grown for the pendulous, trumpet-shaped flowers, 6 in. to 10 in. long. More than 200 blossoms can be open at a single time. Each is suspended from a green, tubular calyx, about half the length of the corolla, which is composed of five fused petals. These bold blossoms shyly nod and appear delicate in shades of pastel pink or yellow. But beware, their nighttime fragrance is intoxicating and will draw you into the exotic garden. Like all parts of this seductive plant, they are poisonous, the instrument of Lucifer, not Gabriel.

Culture: Full sun to dappled shade. Moist, well-drained growing conditions. *Brugmansia* seems to flower heavily with

lunar cycles and likes cool evenings. It peaks in September and October, when flowers are more frequent and last longer.

Height: To 8 ft.

Propagation: Easy from cuttings.

Horticultural use: *Brugmansia* captured the fancy of 19th-century gardeners and is appropriate for the center of Victorian-style lawn beds when the soil is graded into a convex mound higher than the surrounding turf. Train into a standard, and then ring something low around it, like *Alternanthera ficoidea*, that will not interfere with the dangling blossoms. They are good container subjects. When plants are elevated you can peer into their blossoms. However, restricted container roots demand frequent water. Position them in the middle or rear of borders. The delicate fruit of *Duranta erecta* repeats the color of *Brugmansia aurea*.

Overwintering: Specimen tubs or plants dug and potted in late October can be brought into a cool garage or basement until April. Then prune dead wood and gradually expose them to sunlight. Root cuttings in summer and overwinter them on a cool, sunny windowsill for next year's display. Monitor for spider mites. Or purchase new plants from garden centers in May.

Lycianthes rantonnetii
(syn. *Solanum rantonnetii*)
(Blue potato bush)

Origin: Argentina, Paraguay

Decorative interest: This shrub is grown for its bluish purple funnel-shaped flowers, about 1 in. in diameter, that resemble small petunias. They are continuously produced throughout the growing season. Shrubs are often trained into a standard. Lance-shaped leaves, 3 in. to 4 in., are not special.

Culture: Full sun, normal water. Prune hard when needed.

Height: To 6 ft.

Propagation: Stem cuttings.

Horticultural use: Grow as a container specimen or position in the middle or rear of borders. Combine with purple foliage like *Tradescantia pallida* 'Purple Heart', *Tradescantia spathacea*, *Hemigraphis alternata*, or *Strobilanthes dyerianus* and with purple or lavender flowers like *Tibouchina urvilleana* or *Lantana montevidensis*.

Overwintering: Dig, pot, and bring plants indoors to a cool, sunny windowsill, plant room, or greenhouse in mid-October. Prune hard. They are subject to whitefly. Or purchase new Florida-grown plants from garden centers in May.

STRELITZIACEAE

Strelitzia reginae
(Bird of paradise)

Origin: South Africa

Decorative interest: This clump-forming herbaceous plant is grown for its bizarre blue and orange flowers, which resemble some kind of tropical bird in flight. A succession of three-petaled flowers, each up to 6 in. long, emerges from a boat-shaped bract up to 8 in. long on top of a 3-ft.- to 4-ft.-tall stalk. Mature seed-grown plants flower when they are about 6 years old. Exotic-looking spear-shaped leathery leaves, about 1 ft. long, are supported by a petiole up to 3 ft. long. A related species, *Strelitzia nicolai*, the white bird of paradise, has larger, banana-like leaves, over 3 ft. long on top petioles that are even longer. Its similarly shaped flowers are blue and white, but the plant is more often grown for its foliage than its flowers.

Culture: Full sun, normal water. Remove withering leaves at their base. *Strelitzia nicolai* is tolerant of shady conditions.

Height: 2 ft. to 4 ft.; 4 ft. to 8 ft. for *Strelitzia nicolai*.

Propagation: Division of the clump or seed.

Horticultural use: Use as a specimen tub plant or position as a focal plant in the foreground or middle of a border. Position *Strelitzia nicolai* in the rear of borders and use it as a substitute for bananas. Combine *Strelitzia reginae* with the orange flowers of *Cuphea ignea* and the blue flowers of *Clerodendrum ugandense*.

Overwintering: Bring plants indoors to a cool (55°F), sunny windowsill, plant room, or greenhouse in late October. They will survive in a cold but frost-free garage. Older specimens flower more prolifically. Or purchase new plants in May.

VERBENACEAE

Clerodendrum thomsoniae
(Bleeding heart vine, glorybower)

Origin: Tropical western Africa

Decorative interest: This weak-stemmed, viny shrub, is grown both for its habit and its floral display. Flowers, within 5-in. clusters, are composed of a white, bell-shaped calyx from which emerges a bright red tubular corolla, about 1 in. long, that ends in a star. The long-lasting calyx deepens into shades of pink. Dark, glossy green leaves are large, up to 5 in. long. *Clerodendrum splendens* is a similar species with a bright red corolla and a reddish calyx. A hybrid between both species, *C. x speciosum*, resembles *C. thomsoniae* except it has a dull pinkish calyx and a rose-shaded corolla.

Culture: Acclimate to full sun. Normal water. Fertilize when in active growth. Pinch wiry stems to produce denser growth.

Height: 6 in. to 3 ft.

Propagation: Stem cuttings in spring or summer.

Horticultural use: Grow in a hanging basket or let plants cascade from a container. They can also be trained on a vine support in a container. Or directly plant the bleeding heart vine into the foreground of borders. Combine with other red and white colors, like *Hibiscus rosa-sinensis* 'Cooperi'.

Overwintering: Root stem cuttings in summer and grow on a sunny windowsill for next year's garden display. Or dig, pot, and bring plants indoors in mid-October and grow as a houseplant in a sunny, cool window at about 50°F to 55°F. Or purchase new plants in May. They are commonly sold as inexpensive houseplants in small 6-in. pots or larger hanging baskets in most garden centers.

Clerodendrum ugandense (Butterfly bush)

Origin: Tropical Africa

Decorative interest: This erect shrub is grown for its cluster of small, yet beautiful, sky-blue blossoms that are sporadically produced at the end of stems. Four delicate purplish blue stamens protrude and curl outward from the flower. Narrow, 4-in. leaves are elliptic in shape.

Culture: Full sun, normal water.

Height: To 6 ft.

Propagation: Stem cuttings in spring or summer.

Horticultural use: Position one-year plants in the foreground or middle of the border. Older specimens are tall and erect enough to be in the rear. They can act as a vine support for the weak-stemmed *Allamanda*

cathartica; together, the clear yellow and blue are good color contrasts. Achieve a similar effect in a container by using younger, and therefore shorter, plants combined with the shrubby *Allamanda schottii*.

Overwintering: Root stem cuttings in summer and grow on a sunny windowsill for next year's garden display. Or dig, pot, and bring plants indoors in mid-October and grow as a houseplant in a sunny window, plant room, or greenhouse at about 60°F. Or purchase new plants from specialty nurseries in May.

Duranta erecta (syn. *D. repens*) (Golden dewdrop, pigeon berry)

Origin: Tropical America

Decorative interest: This easy-to-grow shrub can be trained into a small tree or topiary. It is grown for diminutive lavender-blue blossoms, less than ½ in. in diameter, that are sporadically produced in clusters up to 6 in. long. Yellow swallowtail butterflies spend hours gathering nectar from them. Persistent golden berries follow and join new flowers that are just opening to create a wonderful color harmony. The cultivar *Duranta erecta* 'Alba' has white flowers.

Culture: Full sun, normal water.

Height: To 6 ft.

Propagation: Stem cuttings.

Horticultural use: Plant large specimens directly into the middle or rear of borders with other complementary golden blossoms, like *Brugmansia aurea*, or golden foliage like *Abutilon pictum* 'Thompsonii'. Grow specimen plants of *Duranta erecta* as a stan-

dard in tubs. Plant young rooted cuttings into the foreground of borders with *Tradescantia pallida* 'Purple Heart' or other burgundy foliage.

Overwintering: Root stem cuttings in summer and grow on a sunny windowsill for next year's garden display. Or dig, pot, and bring plants indoors in mid-October and grow as a houseplant in a sunny window, plant room, or greenhouse. Tolerates 50°F to 55°F, but prefers 60°F to 65°F. Or purchase new plants from specialty nurseries in May.

Lantana camara (Shrub verbena, sage)

Origin: Tropical America

Decorative interest: Short, shrubby plants are grown for the numerous ¼-in. verbena-like flowers that congregate into a domed head the size of a quarter. Flowers appear from summer to frost and are host to bees and butterflies. Colors change from yellow to pink or orange to scarlet. Some cultivars are always white, golden yellow, or orange. Rough, 3-in. leaves are pungent and produced in pairs. *Lantana montevidensis*, the trailing lantana, is a 6-in.-high ground cover species that produces lavender flowers.

Culture: Full sun, normal water. Tolerant of drier conditions. Pinch plants to remain bushy. Or train into a standard. Plants are prone to whitefly.

Height: 1 ft. to 4 ft.; standards are 3 ft. to 5 ft.

Propagation: Easy from cuttings.

Horticultural use: Use standards in formal, architectural situations. Position older specimens into the middle or rear of borders.

Newly propagated plants can go into the foreground of borders, be massed in Victorian-style lawn beds, or be grown in a container. Combine orange-flowering cultivars with *Cuphea ignea* or bronze-foliaged *Alternanthers dentata* 'Rubiginosa'. Match lantana colors with appropriate canna varieties. Yellow-flowered forms are good companions with yellow variegated foliage plants like *Sanchezia speciosa*. Combine *Lantana montevidensis* with *Cuphea hyssopifolia* and *Tradescantia pallida* 'Purple Heart'.

Overwintering: Root cuttings in September and overwinter on a sunny windowsill for next year's display. Or, in October, dig, pot, and bring plants into a bright, cool, but frost-free garage or basement and overwinter at temperatures as low as 40°F. Acclimate to outdoor conditions in April. Prune back dead stems. Or purchase new plants inexpensively at garden centers in May.

ZINGIBERACEAE

Alpinia zerumbet 'Variegata' (syn. *A. speciosa*) (Variegated shell ginger)

Origin: Eastern Asia

Decorative interest: This herbaceous perennial is not grown for its aromatic rhizome, like the true ginger (*Zingiber officinale*) that you grate into culinary delights, but for its highly decorative leaves that are streaked bright yellow. Lance-shaped leaves, over 1 ft. long and 4 in. wide, alternately clasp the stem like that of a waterside reed. Stems emerge erectly, then develop an arching habit. Porcelain-pink flowers are rarely produced in zone 6 gardens.

Culture: Full sun or light shade during the hottest part of the day. They prefer rich, moist organic soil that is slightly acid and can tolerate cooler temperatures. Prune withering stems to the ground.

Height: 2 ft. to 4 ft.

Propagation: Division when needed.

Horticultural use: Position clumps in the foreground of borders near other golden variegated plants like *Sanchezia speciosa*, chartreuse foliage like *Ipomoea batatus* 'Margarita', or yellow flowers like *Pachystacys lutea*. Its arching form makes a good container specimen.

Overwintering: Dig, pot, and bring plants indoors into a warm, sunny greenhouse, plant room, or windowsill in early October. Cut old back stems to the ground to reduce the size of the specimen. In spring, acclimate plants to higher light. As new stems form in sunny conditions, older stems that may have sunburned can be removed to soil level. Or purchase new plants in May. Florida-grown plants are often available in the houseplant section of specialty garden centers.

Costus speciosus 'Variegatus' (Variegated crepe ginger)

Origin: India, Southeast Asia, New Guinea

Decorative interest: This herbaceous perennial is grown for its zebra-like variegated foliage, which adheres to spiraling reddish stems like steps on a staircase. Leaves are up to 10 in. long and have under surfaces soft as velvet. At maturity (but rarely in zone 6 gardens), a cone-like spike of reddish bracts terminates the stem. From the base of each bract, crepe-white flowers emerge for a day.

Culture: Full sun or preferably light shade during the hottest part of the day. They prefer rich, moist organic soil. Use a slow-release fertilizer when planting. Plants do not tolerate dry soil and cool temperatures below 50°F. Prune withering stems to the ground. Plants require support.

Height: To 5 ft.

Propagation: Division of clump or stem cuttings in mist chambers with bottom heat.

Horticultural use: Position in the middle of a border with other variegated plants of similar cultural conditions like *Alocasia macrorrhiza* 'Variegata' or *Hibiscus rosasinensis* 'Cooperi'. Its spiral form contrasts well with the coarse habit of a variegated *Ficus elastica*. Or contrast with the burgundy leaf color of *Colocasia* 'Black Magic'.

Overwintering: Dig, pot, and bring plants into a warm and humid plant room or conservatory in mid-September. This plant is choice and well worth the special coddling it will require. Or order new plants from southern nursery catalogs for late May delivery. They're slow to start until temperatures heat up.

Hedychium coronarium (White butterfly ginger)

Origin: India

Decorative interest: This herbaceous perennial is the most common and easily grown ginger outside of the steamy tropics. It is grown for the flower spike that terminates the growth of stems. White flowers, about 3 in. across, are extraordinarily fragrant in August, September, and October.

Lance-shaped leaves, over 1 ft. long and 4 in. wide, alternately clasp erect stems similarly to *Alpinia* (but they are not variegated). They are distinctly tropical in appearance.

Hedychium gardnerianum, the kahili ginger (photo at left), and *Hedychium coccineum,* the red ginger lily, are larger species with a similar form and have flowers of yellow and red. Numerous *Hedychium* hybrids are worth trying.

Culture: Full sun or light shade during the hottest part of the day. They prefer rich, moist organic soil that is slightly acid and warm, humid conditions but will tolerate cool periods. Prune withering stems to the ground.

Height: 3 ft. to 5 ft.

Propagation: Division of rhizome.

Horticultural use: Position in middle or rear of borders, where their fragrance can be enjoyed. Contrast foliage with that of *Colocasia* cultivars or *Cyperus alternifolius,* which are similar in their cultural requirements. Contrast *H. coccineum* and *H. gard-*

nerianum with bronze foliage plants like *Hibiscus acetosella* 'Red Shield'.

Overwintering: In zone 6 and below, dig *Hedychium coronarium* the first week of November or after a light frost, when you would dig canna rhizomes. Treat them like canna. Wash their beautiful pink rhizomes to remove any soil and let them dry. Then dust with a fungicide and pack the rhizomes in a corrugated cardboard box with dry peat moss, sphagnum moss, sawdust, or excelsior. Store at about 50°F. Pot rhizomes in early April to plant outdoors in late May. Or dig plants in early November, remove old back stems, pot plants, and keep them growing in a warm, sunny plant room or greenhouse until outdoor planting next spring. When the rhizomes are not allowed to dry, plants flower sooner. Zone 7 and 8 gardeners can try to grow *Hedychium* outdoors as a perennial plant.

PHOTO CREDITS

Richard Iversen: acknowledgments page, 9 (bottom), 11, 12, 16, 17, 23 (bottom), 25 (bottom left, bottom right), 26 (left), 32, 33 (right), 35, 40, 44, 46, 49 (right), 51, 53, 59, 60 (left), 61, 62, 63, 65, 70, 71, 74, 75, 77, 79 (left), 82 (left), 83, 86, 87, 88, 90, 93 (left), 94, 95, 97, 101 (left), 103, 104, 111 (bottom), 120 (right), 121, 130 (right), 131, 132, 133, 134 (right), 135 (left, right), 136, 137 (middle, right), 138 (right), 139 (middle, right), 140, 141 (left, right), 142, 144, 145 (left, top right), 146, 147 (left, middle), 148, 149 (left, right), 150 (left, right), 151, 152 (middle, right), 153, 154 (left, right), 155 (left, right), 156, 157, 158 (bottom left, middle, right), 160, 161 (middle, right)

Dency Kane: contents page, 2, 4, 5, 6, 7, 8, 9 (top), 14, 18, 23 (top), 27, 29, 30, 31, 36, 38, 39, 41, 42 (left), 48, 50, 54, 55, 56, 57, 60 (right), 64, 78, 93 (right), 98, 99, 101 (right), 102, 106, 107, 108, 109, 110, 111 (top), 112, 113, 114, 115, 116, 117, 120 (left), 122-123, 125, 126, 130 (middle), 139 (left), 145 (bottom right), 158 (top left), 159 (right), 165

Derek Fell: 10, 21, 25 (top), 33 (left), 37 (bottom), 82 (right), 84, 89, 130 (right), 134 (middle), 135 (middle), 138 (middle), 152 (left), 154 (middle), 161 (left), 162

Pamela J. Harper: 37 (top), 42 (right), 79 (right), 85, 134 (left), 137 (left), 138 (left), 141 (middle), 143 (middle, right), 147 (right), 150 (middle), 155 (middle), 159 (left)

Ken Druse: 13, 19, 24, 26 (right), 80-81, 100, 149 (middle)

Alan and Linda Detrick ©1999: 82 (top), 91, 119

Anthony Tesselaar International: 49 (left), 143 (left)

Sean Carrington: 20

Scala/Art Resource, New York: 28

Netherlands Flower Bulb Information Center: 124

Appendix: Annual Plants of Tropical Origin to Combine with Tropical Plants

It is common to find annual plants growing in gardens within the tropics; many of them are native to tropic environments, and their cultural requirements are similar. Annuals and tropicals look good together and have been combined in bedding displays since the 19th century. To my eyes, they are a more harmonious pair than tropical plants with most perennials or shrubs. The following annual plants are those I like to combine with the tropical plants included in the glossary.

Botanical Name	Common Name	Botanical Name	Common Name
Amaranthus caudatus	Love-lies-bleeding	*Nicotiana sylvestris*	
Amaranthus tricolor	Tampala	*Pennisetum setaceum* 'Purpureum' (syn. *P. rueppellii*)	Fountain grass
Angelonia angustifolia			
Bassia scoparia trichophylla (syn. *Kochia trichophylla*)	Burning bush	*Pennisetum villosum* (syn. *P. longistylum*)	
Begonia semperflorens	Wax begonia	*Perilla frutescens* 'Atropurpurea'	
Browallia speciosa	Bush violet	*Petunia*	
Capsicum annuum	Chili pepper	*Salvia coccinea*	
Catharanthus roseus	Madagascar periwinkle	*Salvia leucantha*	Mexican bush sage
Celosia argentea cristata	Cockscomb	*Salvia splendens*	Scarlet sage
Celosia argentea plumosa	Plume cockscomb	*Senecio cineraria*	Dusty miller
Cosmos bipinnatus		*Solenostemon scutellarioides*	Coleus
Cosmos sulphureus		*Tagetes erecta*	African marigolds
Fuchsia triphylla		*Tagetes patula*	French marigolds
Helianthus annuus	Sunflower	*Tithonia rotundifolia*	Mexican sunflower
Heliotropium arborescens	Heliotrope	*Torenia fournieri*	Wishbone flower
Impatiens balsamina	Rose balsam	*Tropaeolum majus*	Nasturtium
Impatiens hawkeri	New Guinea impatiens	*Verbena* x *hybrida*	
Impatiens walleriana	Busy lizzy	*Zinnia elegans*	
Melampodium paludosum 'Medallion'		*Zinnia haageana* (syn. *Z. angustifolia*)	Mexican zinnia
Nicotiana alata (syn. *N. affinis*)	Flowering tobacco		

Sources

Tropical plants are common in American nurseries as landscape plants in Florida, Texas, and California or as houseplants in the northern states. They are sold in grocery stores, home stores, and garden centers all year long, but a greater variety appear in springtime when they are marketed as summer patio plants. For special varieties of tropicals, check the following sources:

Angel Plants (Wholesale)
560 Deer Park Avenue
Dix Hills, NY 11746
(516) 242-7788

Logee's Greenhouses
141 North Street
Danielson, CT 06239
(860) 774-8038

The Banana Tree
715 Northhampton Street
Easton, PA 18042
(610) 253-9589

Plumeria People
910 Leander Drive
Leander, TX 78641
(512) 259-0807

Glasshouse Works
Church Street
Stewart, OH 45778-0097
(800) 837-2142

Stokes Tropicals
P.O. Box 9868
New Iberia, LA 70562-9868
(800) 624-9706

Landcraft Environments (Wholesale)
1160 East Mill Road
Mattituck, NY 11952-1289
(516) 298-3510

K. Van Vourgondien & Sons
245 Route 109
P.O. Box 1000
Babylon, NY 11702
(800) 552-9996

Bibliography

Bannochie, I., and M. Light. *Gardening in the Caribbean.* London: Macmillan Press, 1993.

Bar-Zvi, D. *Tropical Gardening.* New York: Pantheon Books, 1996.

Brickell, C., & J. Zuk. *The American Horticultural Society A-Z Encyclopedia of Garden Plants.* New York: DK Publishing, 1997.

Courtright, G. *Tropicals.* Portland, Ore.: Timber Press, 1988.

Graf, A. B. *Exotic Plant Manual* (5th ed.). Rutherford, N.J.: Roehrs Co., 1978.

Graf, A. B. *Tropica: Color Cyclopia of Exotic Plants and Trees* (4th ed.). Rutherford, N.J.: Roehrs Co., 1992.

Hibberd, S. *New and Rare Beautiful-Leaved Plants.* London: Bell and Daldy, 1870.

Holttum, R. E., & I. Enoch. *Gardening in the Tropics.* Portland, Ore.: Timber Press, 1991.

Jerome, K. *Indoor Gardening.* New York: Pantheon Books, Knopf Publishing Group, 1995.

Martin, T. *Once upon a Windowsill: A History of Indoor Plants.* Portland, Ore.: Timber Press, 1988.

Martin, T. *Well-Clad Windowsills: Houseplants for Four Exposures.* New York: Macmillan, 1994.

Robinson, W. *The Subtropical Garden or Beauty of Form in the Flower Garden* (2nd ed.). London: John Murray, 1879.

Walker, J. *The Subtropical Garden.* Portland, Ore.: Timber Press, 1996.

Warren, W. *The Tropical Garden.* New York: Thames and Hudson, 1997.

Warren, W. *Tropical Plants for Home and Garden.* New York: Thames and Hudson, 1997.

Watkins, J., & T. Sheehan. *Florida Landscape Plants: Native and Exotic.* Gainsville, Fla.: The University Presses of Florida, 1975.

Index

Publisher: *Jim Childs*

Associate Publisher: *Helen Albert*

Editorial Assistant: *Cherilyn DeVries*

Editor: *Peter Chapman*

Designer: *Henry Roth*

Layout Artist: *Lynne Phillips*

Illustrator: *Peter Eckert*

Typefaces: *Legacy, Galliard*

Paper: *80-lb. Utopia Two Gloss*

Printer: *R. R. Donnelley, Willard, Ohio*